Moment to Moment

A positive approach to managing classroom behavior

Joey Mandel

Foreword:

Joanne Cummings

Pembroke Publishers Limited

© 2013 Pembroke Publishers
538 Hood Road
Markham, Ontario, Canada L3R 3K9
www.pembrokepublishers.com

Distributed in the U.S. by Stenhouse Publishers
480 Congress Street
Portland, ME 04101
www.stenhouse.com

We acknowledge the financial support of the Government of Canada through the
Canada Book Fund (CBF) for our publishing activities.

We acknowledge the assistance of the Government of Ontario through the Ontario
Media Development Corporation's Ontario Book Initiative.

Library and Archives Canada Cataloguing in Publication

Mandel, Joey, author
    Moment to moment : a positive approach to managing classroom behaviour / Joey
Mandel.
Includes bibliographical references and index.

Issued in print and electronic formats.
ISBN 978-1-55138-287-6 (pbk.).-- ISBN 978-1-55138-855-7 (pdf)

    1. Behavior modification. 2. Classroom management. I. Title.

LB1060.2.M36 2013   370.15'28   C2013-904237-7
                                               C2013-904238-5

Editor: Kat Mototsune
Cover Design: John Zehethofer
Typesetting: Jay Tee Graphics Ltd.

Printed and bound in Canada
9 8 7 6 5 4 3 2 1

MIX
Paper from
responsible sources
FSC
www.fsc.org   FSC® C004071

Contents

Foreword

I first met Joey Mandel through my work as a clinical child psychologist. Joey was a concerned teacher and, as we consulted about a particular case, I made the point that the child would need "moment-to-moment support" in the classroom in order to develop social skills. I learned this concept from my mentor Dr. Debra Pepler, Scientific Co-Director of PREVNet (Promoting Relationships and Eliminating Violence). At the mention of moment-to-moment support, Joey's eyes lit up. She intuitively understood that the classroom teacher is ideally placed to take advantage of the naturally occurring moments during day-to-day activities to nurture a child's ability to interact with others and adapt successfully to classroom routines.

Thus began a long series of conversations with Joey, who was determined to more fully understand how children develop the complex set of motor, language, social, emotional, and cognitive skills that are necessary to thrive at school and, indeed, in life. As an experienced teacher, Joey clearly understood that a positive learning environment in the classroom had to start with a web of respectful, caring, and inclusive relationships among its members. She had already made the switch from "teaching the curriculum" to teaching individual children. Joey relentlessly pursued current research and theory in child development in order to enhance her understanding of why some children struggle socially and behaviorally. This understanding became the foundation for her comprehensive model of moment-to-moment support that is so beautifully described in this book.

Indeed, there are a number of children in every classroom who are not able to meet age-appropriate expectations for emotional and behavioral regulation, social interaction, or learning. Without relying on diagnostic labels, Joey focuses on addressing these children's social skill deficits. Joey is deeply committed to the principle that children misbehave when they lack the skills to do better. This led her to become a true expert in "unpacking" a child's problematic behavior to identify the underlying reasons. Joey has formulated a remarkable, scientifically based framework that enables teachers to carefully observe, reflect, identify, and address critical skill deficits. Moreover, Joey is an expert in communicating these ideas through detailed descriptions in simple, user-friendly language. Teachers can use Joey's Class Survey to customize social-emotional learning goals for individual students while positively influencing the group dynamics of the class as a whole.

Perhaps most exciting, however, is Joey's creativity in designing or adapting games and learning activities that target specific social skills. This book provides a very rich compendium of learning activities designed to promote growth across the wide domain of relevant social skills, while enhancing children's feelings of enjoyment, belonging, and accomplishment. Written by an experienced classroom teacher for other classroom teachers, they exhibit Joey's superb sense of what is both doable and effective in fostering social skill growth. Using Joey's detailed description of the games, before and after discussion points, and suggestions for the extra supports that some students will require, teachers can easily incorporate these activities into their everyday practice.

I was fortunate to watch these games in action a few years ago when Joey ran a summer camp program in her backyard. Two of my clients were participating, and I was deeply impressed to see how well they were able to apply their new skills in a small-group setting. What stayed with me was the joy and confidence I saw on the faces of children who had previously struggled to stay behaviorally regulated and who had shied away from peers. This is why Joey's games and activities are so important—they ensure that all children are included in safe, real-world, social learning opportunities that are relevant, growth-enhancing, and fun.

I am thrilled that Joey has shared her learning, formidable creativity, and dedication to social-emotional learning through writing this book. My greatest hope is that teachers will use the moment-to-moment framework and learning activities regularly throughout the school year. This will promote all children's social skills, and ultimately enhance their capacity for healthy relationships throughout their lives. We can offer our children no greater gift.

—Joanne Cummings, Ph.D., C.Psych
  Psychologist, Blue Balloon Health Services
  Director of Knowledge Mobilization, PREVNet

Preface

About four years ago, I was given a book called *The Explosive Child* by Ross W. Greene that was for me the beginning of a paradigm shift in teaching and parenting. Dr. Greene writes that sometimes there is more going on than a child being disruptive and defiant. If we look a little deeper and seek to understand what is going on, and help the child explain him- or herself and the situation, then maybe we can come up with a plan that lets everyone move forward happily. His model of collaborative problem-solving can help get us through challenging moments and find solutions to difficult behavior.

Difficult behavior tells us that the child doesn't have the necessary skills to respond to a particular environment (Greene, 2005) and that if we, as teachers and parents, come in very quickly, very strictly, and in a harsh way, we escalate the problem so the child shuts down and becomes even more inflexible. So what are these skills and how do they affect behavior? I looked to Till Davy, who has done a significant amount of research on executive function disorders and the domains of development. Dr. Davy indicates that metaphors of the executive and regulatory functioning parts of the brain as "the CEO of the brain" or the "conductor of an orchestra" are misleading, as they lead us to believe that all that is required in order for a child's executive functioning to improve is that they "try harder" (Davy, 2011). In fact, the executive and regulatory functioning parts of the brain are a much more complex system of automatic guides that monitor, control, inhibit, prompt, guide, balance, cue, check, and correct our perceptions, our emotions, our thinking, our memory, and our actions.

Though the five domains of this book are not the same as Davy's five domains (this book does not have the executive function domain), the skill-based focus shares a similar foundation.

So I had an understanding that behind behavior there are skills in various domains of development that influence a child's behavior; that, in reaction to difficult moments, I need to slow myself down and empathize with the child, find out how the child is struggling.

I loved this newfound information, but there were two problems. First, most of the children I work with are too young to know why they struggle. This lack of awareness of their triggers and their inability to articulate their problems are, in fact, among the things they struggle with! Secondly, as a teacher, I need a way not only to support the child in crisis situations or meltdowns, but also to help build those weak skills so the child will be less often in crisis. This is where I found a perfect fit with the work of Michelle Garcia Winner and her concept of Social Thinking®, the ability to think about the intentions, motives, and prior knowledge of others in a social situation. In my mind, Michelle Garcia Winner's greatest contribution is her examination of how people share space with others. Throughout this book, the verbal thinking cues and references to sharing social space are based in the social awareness and thinking strategies of Social Thinking.

Social Thinking provides excellent vocabulary for many of the social-emotional skills this book addresses.

But it is not all about thinking. It is not enough for a child to think about a new way of acting and then for the child to be able to apply that thinking successfully in the moment. Remember, as adults we know the areas in which we struggle, and yet we ourselves are not always able to modify our own behavior, no matter how hard we try. Helping children achieve what we are telling them to do is the most difficult, yet crucial, final step. This process takes time and empathetic support in the moment, and needs to be detailed step-by-step for teachers.

And so emerged this book. Teachers need support, guidance, help, and tools to deal with their students' behavior issues day in and day out. It is not enough to tell a teacher to be kind to his/her class, work to the needs of the class, and make sure that all the children are nice to each other. In a class of thirty children, working together day in and day out, learning multiple different subjects at multiple ability levels, this is something that is very hard to achieve. What this book suggests is how you can find better insight, awareness, and empathy into the causes of these behaviors by understanding the behavior as a skill challenge, rather than misbehavior. It shows you concrete options for exactly what you can do in the moment to support your students in developing skills they will use for the rest of their lives.

—Joey Mandel

Acknowledgments

This book would likely be just another file on my computer were it not for my friends' and family's consistent encouragement and belief. I am very lucky to have an amazing support group and many people in my life to call great friends. This book was written by me, but comes from the feedback, insight, and knowledge from the people with whom I share teaching and parenting experiences and stories. I would like to thank all the families who welcomed me into their homes, played games with me, and shared their experiences—they are the foundation of this book. Thanks to Jennifer Cumming and Marsha Hamilton at St. Clement's Early Learning School, both natural pro-social teachers. To my good friends who took the time to read the book and give me their thoughts and ideas, I am especially grateful to Christine Lenouvel, Lisa Byrne, Hannah Sung, Fran Clark, Jeannie Melardi, Leah-Ann Lymer, Laura Cornish, Sophie Awai, Linda Hiraki, Nancy Ng, Jennifer Wigmore, Lauren Speer, Ilaria Sheikh, Shira Katzberg, Sarah Waldman, Melissa Frew, and Jill Sanderson. At Pembroke, Mary Macchiusi's direction and persistence has been invaluable and Kat Mototsune's hard work and great skill were instrumental in shaping the final version and making it a much better book. Jill Farber, Cat White, Lauren Baker, Ida Marissen, and Joan Gardiner are early intervention specialists at the top of their field who taught me all I know, and supported me while they did it. To Ian Roth I owe many thanks for the comments on the games, but also for his fountain of knowledge and reassurance during my own learning journey. Thanks to Joanne Cummings for her unwavering enthusiasm. To Ginnelle Elliott and Frank Sawyer, thank you for your constant praise, edits, and laughs. This book would never have been completed were it not for my dad's complete belief in it and my mom's complete belief in me, as they both spent hours not only talking about it, but reading each new version I wrote. And finally, thanks to my husband and my two boys, who have made me the happiest I have ever been and teach me every day.

Introduction

Teachers' college has one main focus and communicates three messages. The main focus is the curriculum. Pre-service teachers are taught how to teach language, run guided-reading circles, use manipulatives for math, and set up science experiments. In the background of these detailed curriculum lesson plans are three consistent messages: classroom management is the key to a teacher's success; teachers will teach in inclusive classrooms and need to teach to the needs of all students; bullying will not be tolerated. The curriculum lessons are taught explicitly and in detail to the teachers. But for the other three messages, all the knowledge is implied.

It cannot be assumed that all teachers know how to help a child whose behavior is challenging without using authoritarian means or singling out the child so that peers judge the child's behavior. Teachers need to be explicitly taught techniques and strategies to create a non-judgmental classroom social climate when dealing with such children.

When I look back at my first year of teaching, I see how hard it is to attain the delicate balance of maintaining classroom control without using a negative approach. Since I was well-trained and prepared in the curriculum, my classroom dynamic and priorities became centred on ensuring I covered it extensively and properly. My prep time and teaching revolved around the curriculum; everything else was an interruption to the lesson of the day and the material that needed to be covered. I was so busy teaching the material, how much time did I have to think about the children whose behavior showed they were having trouble? With some, the nuances of their social behavior did not affect the progression of my lessons, so their social struggles did not always catch my attention. But where the behavior of the student interrupted the lesson and affected the learning of other children, my focus on the behavior of the child was based on my need to get on with the lesson. Instead of supporting the needs of the child who struggled with behavior, I would sometimes use quick negative reinforcement to get the child back on task. Repeated negative reinforcement—singling out the child in frustration, correcting the child in front of peers, and telling the child to get back on task when he/she has no idea how to perform the task—might gain us classroom control, but does so by creating an atmosphere of intolerance. If we send a message that what the child is doing is bad, over time other children will start correcting and alienating that child. The teacher can inadvertently start a cycle of behavior that is intolerant of the individual behavior challenges of the children in the class.

It is not a supreme ability to teach math or fabulous life experience that makes a strong teacher. The most influential commodity a teacher brings to the classroom is his or her own positive personal qualities and warm character in the face of challenging situations. The individual teacher's daily modeling of an openness to the ideas of others, optimistic attitude, acceptance of all students, tolerance of mistakes, patience throughout challenging moments, and inclusion for everyone may be the strongest teaching tool to help shape positive behaviors in children and influence the way they treat each other and learn. A pro-social teacher is one who understands that she or he plays a crucial role in teaching social-emotional curriculum, then supports and guides that curriculum all day long in the classroom.

Meet the Children

Sometimes the best way to identify what needs doing is to look at the behavior in action. Here are four students who will be returned to throughout this book. Try to see the behaviors of your own students in these profiles. It will help you target which strategies can help you manage your own classroom, moment to moment.

Jenny

It starts right from drop off. All the children are gathered on the playground, ready to go inside. But Jenny is off by herself, near the fence, trying to place leaves in a hole in the ground. When the school bell rings, she does not move. Her mother approaches her, calling her name. When she reaches Jenny, she bends down and touches her shoulder. Jenny jumps up in surprise, as if her mom came out of nowhere. The negotiation and battle begin. Jenny is unmovable. Reasoning does not work; counting down has no impact; threats are ignored. Finally, Jenny's mom pulls Jenny up, and Jenny immediately goes into an intense state of resistance, moving toward her mom then away from her, moaning, lying on the ground.

In Junior Kindergarten, the teacher often finds Jenny crouched under a little table in the back of the room, as if there is danger in the class. When leaving the classroom, Jenny will not line up. The gym teacher reports that one time Jenny just left the line-up into the gym and he couldn't find her. In Senior Kindergarten Jenny needs one-on-one teacher cueing and reminders to complete her work at, and sometimes slightly above, grade level. She needs reminders to attend to her work and to focus on the activity. Through Grade 1, Jenny never brings in her school forms. Her backpack is always a mess and she forgets her lunch most days.

Neil

Neil's behavior struggles affect his ability to function in school each day; his parents advocate for their son with a level of authority and righteousness that would leave any teacher feeling demoralized and defensive. The list of classroom strategies and accommodations for Neil would require the work of three teachers.

The Grade 4 teacher, in anticipation of Neil's behavior, takes a harsh and unforgiving line with Neil. Yet Neil's behavior gets worse. Neil walks into the class like he owns the place. His voice dominates the room, his reactions even stronger, sharper, and more aggressive than before. He demands attention and moves through the classroom like a bulldozer. His outbursts, meltdowns, and verbal statements increase in both intensity and harshness. In play with other children, he seems unaware that they have feelings too. He grabs and takes; worse, he does not seem to notice when another child is sad or hurt—their crying upsets him. Other children move away from him, scared or just unsure. He does not seem to speak to other children; instead, he is always calling the teacher to tell what the other children are doing to annoy him or what they should not be doing.

Marsha

Marsha is gifted academically, but is considered socially awkward and different from the other children. At recess, she runs around, appearing to play a game by herself. By Grade 6, group work is becoming harder and harder for Marsha. Her group members like working with her, since she is a great project leader and always knows everything about the subject. But more and more, working with Marsha means doing everything Marsha wants. If at any point someone else has a different idea or opinion, Marsha becomes very upset. Her body tenses up and she forcefully argues with the group for her ideas. If the group decides, with a vote and group consensus, to do a project in another way, Marsha refuses to participate in the rest of the assignment.

The teacher begins to notice other behaviors from Marsha. Marsha seems to come into class more agitated than before. She walks around a lot before sitting down, bumping into things and other students. She gets out of her seat during desk work to get a tissue or refill her water bottle, and sometimes leaves the class without explanation. She tells her teacher that she feels the other children are not being nice to her and do not like her. Marsha seems to approach students more than she did before, but does it by coming right into their space and interrupting the conversation. Marsha asks the other children to play her game, often when they are already in the middle of an activity. When the children politely tell Marsha that they do not want to switch games, she continues to insist that they play her game.

Lee

Everyone loves Lee, a lively Grade 1 student, imaginative, full of life, and wonderfully energetic. Adults and teachers are always impressed with his funny sayings and his dramatic flair. Yet in class, Lee needs constant reminders to sit still, to walk slowly, not to dump papers off the desk. Lee can't be in the house centre for more than two minutes without another child complaining about him and the intensity with which he plays. He will take toys from another child without asking. If another child wants a turn with a toy, Lee's whole body shakes; he holds the toys close as if they were the last toys in the room. He will scream at the other child, sometimes pushing or hitting. At carpet time, Lee either stares down at a spot on the carpet or lies down on the carpet and pushes his body against another child. Despite the fact that Lee's vocabulary is superior and he even seems to know some French and Spanish (perhaps from TV), he never seems to talk while playing with other children. He grabs toys, pushes his way into play and around the room, and grunts most of his communication to his peers. Lee has never once been heard telling a story or explaining something. He seldom asks questions and will not volunteer to answer questions. When asked a question, he appears nervous and unsure. His main response to verbal questions is "I don't know." Yet his teacher has heard Lee talking nonstop to his parents.

A Social-Emotional Curriculum

So how does one teacher stop Lee from moving around the room all day and Neil from dominating the room? How does one teacher get Marsha to listen to what her group wants and Jenny to come to school ready to learn? How can you gain classroom control and teach to the high needs of these four students, much less the rest of the class? The reality of the school system is that a teacher will have all four of these kids in each class, along with 18 to 20 others who bring their own unique needs, strengths, and challenges.

There are many books that provide excellent strategies to build a collaborative and inclusive classroom. But some of them miss the hard stuff. They are missing the big problem. In truth, there is no quick fix for Neil. No matter how positive, supportive, and accepting a teacher is of Neil, he is going to mess up time and time again throughout the year. He is going to wreck a well-planned lesson and he might bang into another child, most likely on purpose. There will be many times when Marsha will refuse to slow down with her ideas and she is going to get upset in class, she is going to be rigid in her thinking and she is going to walk away from children who do not listen to her. Jenny will forget her backpack; she will come to school without the item that each child needs to complete an art project. And Lee is going to walk up to a group of kids and grab their toys.

Compare this with other aspects of learning—for example, when a child struggles to read no one gets upset with the child. We do not blame the parents. We protect the child in class; we do not ask that child to read out loud; we do not have her read books that are at grade level; and on creative writing assignments, we might pair her up with a student who could scribe. We would not tolerate another child laughing at her or calling her stupid. There is a schoolwide plan in place to help the slow reader. The teachers know how to assess the child and can begin a reading intervention program. They send reading activities home to the parents and might advise getting a tutor. It does not mean that the child will learn how to read quickly, but no one would expect her to be able to.

We do not have this kind of plan for the social-emotional curriculum. Teachers don't receive mental-health training. If they take special education courses, they learn about diagnoses and labels; however, the terms are very general and at most explain what the child can't do. Dyslexia tells us that a child can't read; that is the first step in teaching that child how to read.

When a child repeatedly does not comply with social norms of behavior, we may label that child with Asperger's/Autism Spectrum Disorder (ASD), Attention Deficit Hyperactivity Disorder (ADHD), Obsessive-Compulsive Disorder (OCD), Oppositional Defiance Disorder (ODD), or a Nonverbal Learning Disability (NLD). The disorder is given as the reason for a child's inability to comply. School boards give teachers a brief definition of the labels. They indicate that the teacher must treat and assess this student differently, that the teacher must accept that the student's behavior will be different. This is our expectation of an inclusive classroom with a teacher teaching to different needs. What is not explained is how to teach a particular child differently, why the behavior is different, which behaviors to make allowances for and which are within the student's control, and what to do to help that student. What is missing is the training, insight, and information that would allow a teacher to build that student's skills, instead of giving the student a pass for often-inappropriate behavior.

In my years of working with children, some with diagnoses and some without, I made two observations. First, I noticed that the behavior of the child with the diagnosis was not consistent. A child with a speech and language delay who struggled with social communication was able to ask for a toy, tell a story, and engage in a back-and-forth conversation with a friend in a calm environment. Yet at school, this child hardly ever spoke: stuttered when he talked and used, at best, one-word utterances when he wanted something. This kind of inconsistency is

A recent Ontario survey indicated that most teachers (92%) reported that they had children in their class dealing with mental-health challenges, yet 93.3% indicated that they feel unprepared to help students with mental-health problems. (Andrews, 2013)

the reason why some parents are unable to accept that their child needs help; the child's behavior might actually differ at home and at school. It is also the reason why we perceive that a child chooses to behave a certain way.

The second thing I noticed was that diagnoses are not consistent with behavior. Over the years, I found that my individualized programs for each child did not fall into categories of diagnosis. I did not run the same social program for all the children I worked with who had ADHD. Some of the children who did not have a diagnosis had the exact same program as a child with ASD, despite the fact that another child with ASD needed a separate program. If I was not using the diagnosis to drive my programming, what was I using? Each child I worked with had a skill-based intervention program. The skills were based on observation sessions I had with the child, instead of on a diagnosis.

What do these two observations lead us to? The fact is that difficult behavior does not usually occur because the child is "behavioral" or attention-seeking. It is not caused by a lack of motivation, poor parenting, or a lack of discipline. Teachers need to understand the behavior of a child in the context of what that behavior reveals about the child's social-emotional skill development. Once a teacher understands what these skill deficits are, some of these skills can actually be taught and built. Some children need extra help and patience in the classroom while they build these skills, including perspective-taking, social reciprocity, attention, flexibility, and behavior modulation. These skills are abstract in nature and situationally based, so they are hard to define and classify, and are not seen in behaviors exhibited all the time and in all environments. Not having these skills affects a child's social world as much as dyslexia affects a child's reading. And, like reading, these are skills that need to be better understood and then worked on over time, through teaching and practice.

Through information and knowledge, this book seeks to empower teachers to know what learning skills lie behind clusters of behaviors and how these issues influence social-emotional development. If a teacher is more aware of common patterns of behavior, he or she will know what to be paying attention to and, perhaps most importantly, how to support the social-emotional learning of particular students. Teachers equipped with a strong understanding of these skills deficits will be able to more effectively guide children in the moment.

Using this Book

Once teachers have a better understanding of the social-emotional skill deficits a child might face, they need to be equipped with a process for supporting the student. All teachers can positively support students, guide them, and help them. But in order to effectively influence the learning success of a child with a skill-deficit, the teacher needs to have an awareness of the external and internal causes of the behavior, to understand what different behaviors are telling them about a child's social-emotional skill-deficit profile, to recognize what these skill deficits look like and how the skills can, in fact, be taught. All of this will put the teacher in a position to be able to know how to support this child in the moment.

Teachers and the school itself needs a well-developed plan that includes four important steps:

- **Looking Beyond the Behavior** to understand what specific behaviors and their triggers reveal about the social-emotional skill deficits of a child.

- **Understanding Social-Emotional Skills** by type, assessing what skill deficits underlie specific behaviors, and planning how these skills can be taught.
- **Active Skill Development** by introducing the skills in classroom activities.
- **Moment-to-Moment Support** of individual students practicing the social-emotional skills.

1

Supporting Students Moment to Moment

In the Introduction, I compared reading challenges to social challenges and argued that we need to be able to more systematically support social intervention the way we support reading intervention. I do not pretend that this comparison is without fault. When it comes to that child with dyslexia, her specific skill weakness is clear and its impact on her learning is obvious, as is what should be done about it. We modify (change) her work, then we accommodate (support) her while she does it. We do this because she learns differently from her peers. We can do this while being equitable to her and still be equitable to others. She can do different work and it does not take away from the work of another child. But when it comes to a social-emotional skill, equity is more complicated. Social interactions involve other children. A child's social-emotional skill deficit itself affects other children, in a group or in the whole class. Modifying (changing) the rules for one child also affects other children.

Altering social expectations, rules, routines, for a child with different social, emotional, and behavioral challenges blurs the boundaries between fair and unfair. This dilemma is not restricted to the classroom. When we see a child having a massive meltdown in swimming lessons, at the grocery store, or at a party, few people think, "Poor kid, he must have a different means of modulating his emotional regulation. Everyone should take a deep breath, slow down, and get down to his level. We should listen to his story and figure out what is going on with him today, in this setting, in these lessons. If the teenaged swim coach could simply modify her behavior toward the child, she will help him regulate." A more common thought is that the parents need to be stricter and more consistent with the child, and that the kid should start acting appropriately for his age.

Herein lies an important point. In general, it is unfair to modify and change the rules and expectations for one child. That does not mean that it will never have to be done, but it is very hard to maintain different rules for different children; in the long run, it rarely proves helpful for the child with the skill deficit. But it is not unfair to accommodate and support each child so that he or she can be successful in achieving the rule or expectation.

We don't always have to change the rule; we might just have to give the child more time, cues, and help to get there. If we put in the support systems to help a child with a weak skill, the child will be more successful in accomplishing the task.

Looking Beyond the Behavior

In the Introduction we met four children. Aspects of these four children might be seen in many of the children in every class. No two children are exactly the same but, if we look closely enough, we can begin to see common patterns and profiles. Their behavior that we observe daily in class begins to represent challenges to their social-emotional skills.

Whether or not a child is academically at grade level is not relevant to the social, emotional, and behavioral skills a teacher can begin to record anecdotally and can look for in order to develop a profile of the child.

What lies behind the behavior of these children? What explains some of these odd, controlling, overpowering, inflexible, mean, hyper, or disorganized behaviors?

We need to look at why Jenny
- stares at her pencil all morning in math class
- has difficulty doing or completing non-preferred activities
- was slow to learn to ride a bike
- is messy and/or disorganized
- seems tired or slow
- seems not to listen
- plays for a long time with one toy or object
- does not ask a lot of questions
- rarely initiates play with others
- tends to play with particular toys in a repetitive manner
- avoids eye contact

And why Neil
- is angry and resentful
- is irritable
- wants nothing to do with friends or family
- defies and refuses to comply with others
- has many temper outbursts
- has moods that change quickly and to extremes
- looks unhappy for no clear reason
- gets upset if someone makes too much noise
- does not appear to be sad if someone else is sad or hurt
- seems to complain about everything and everyone
- does not seem satisfied in the moment and always wants something else or something better
- complains to adults about the behavior of other children

And why Marsha
- needs everything to be a particular way
- frightens easily
- avoids certain social situations
- is fussy about cleanliness
- has many fears
- is distracted by noises around her
- has difficulty in crowds
- gets upset if someone rearranges her things

And why Lee
- is clumsy
- is always on the go
- trips a lot
- makes friends but loses them easily
- is restless and overactive
- is happy to see friends, but then does not follow up and play with them
- fails to finish things he starts

- blurts out answers to questions before the questions have been completed
- demands things right away
- bumps into other kids
- grabs objects out of other children's hands

The Trigger

Before we begin to examine the behavior, we need to look back and consider what led up to the behavior: the trigger. This is sometimes called the cause, the antecedent, or the stimulus, but is simply the reason that the child is acting and behaving the way he/she is in the moment. When children are doing what they want, in an environment they are comfortable in, they are most likely happy and easy-going. When a child is at home, watching TV and eating ice cream, we don't see any of these behaviors! Children exhibit challenging, odd, or inappropriate behaviors when they are ill-prepared to deal with a trigger situation because they lack the skills to handle the situation (Greene, 2005).

It is important to attempt to get a good sense of the behaviors—where, when, and with whom they appear. If, for example, a child does not like to do math, examine what it is about math that he does not like, what he would need in order to make math class more successful. Then you can come up with a strategy that would decrease challenging behavior around math class. What if the real reason he is always disruptive in math class is that it is the period before lunch and he is hungry, and you could pre-empt his difficult behavior by making sure he had a bigger snack? What if that math class was hard because kids came in from another class and the room was much louder and noisier? Sometimes it is easier to change the volume of the whole class than to chase a child's negative behavior through the lesson because he is bothered by noise.

Other triggers are just as important to figure out, but are not as easy to solve. For example, if the noise, unpredictability, and open space of recess overwhelms a child and causes her to shut down, we need to have a better understanding of the skills most children would use to handle and cope with that environment. Why is it that this child is unable to cope with the challenges that life throws at all of us? In most cases, we can't change recess, but if we have a better understanding of the skill deficits that make this child ill-prepared to deal with recess, we will know where to focus our energy. We can develop a better toolkit of strategies to help the child. Instead of telling her to "go play at recess and have fun," we will be helping her develop the skills necessary for her to do that.

This situationality does not apply only to Neil's meltdowns and negative behavior. Behaviors like tripping, banging into other children, and wanting to control play are also often not seen across all environments and situations. Lee might be slower and calmer at home. He might sit for longer and read a book on the couch. He does not bang around excitedly and move his arms all about. He might speak more and be able to hold a conversation. The behaviors that appear to be so much a part of who this child is might be seen only at school.

Jenny

Jenny hides under the table because she has sensory challenges. As the noise of the room overwhelms her, it acts as her trigger. Her instinctive fight-or-flight reaction leads her to hide under a table and slow down her movements.

Neil

Neil reacts strongly to negative emotion and to authority; the more the teacher mirrors his behavior, the more disruptive he becomes.

The point is not to always eliminate triggers from a child's environment. Schools have rules, routines, and expectations, and so does the real world. Removing all things that upset a child will not help that child develop the skills needed to face those challenges.

Marsha

When a classmate's behavior goes against a rule or belief of Marsha's, her reaction is more intense and self-righteous than that of most children. Because of the rigidity of Marsha's thought process, in her mind her reaction is not out of proportion with the seriousness of the trigger.

Lee

When Lee is asked a direct question, it causes him stress and shuts dowon his ability to access language. He quickly says, "I don't know" or answers with minimal information.

Understanding Social-Emotional Skills

If some children are ill-prepared to deal with certain situations because they lack the skills needed to cope with them, we have to look at childhood developmental skills and how they affect a child's behavior. This book examines five commonly used, broad categories of development: physical, language, social, emotional, and cognitive.

There is a sequence of development that occurs on a continuum for all children. Children acquire these skills at different ages. Yet the development of these skills is crucial for the expectations that society places on children. Children are expected to be able to cope with certain situations and perform certain tasks by specific ages. A child's experiences and exposure influence the rate of development: this means that the development of different children can be typical and still show considerable variations. A very wide range of normal development includes slow and atypical development of skills. Sometimes, despite enriched experiences and nurtured exposure, a child is slow to acquire skills and, in play and social interaction, begins to exhibit behavioral signs not consistent with his or her chronological age.

Some children's struggles are so pervasive that the child misses many clear developmental milestones. Early in such a child's life, parents, teachers, and doctors are able to identify that the child needs help and can begin a specific process of early intervention. There are relatively effective ways of identifying low-functioning children and services available for them; however, we are not learning from the experiences of these children and applying what we know to children whose challenges in similar skills are in a much milder form. There are many children in regular nursery schools and elementary schools whose skills are not weak enough that they are diagnosed with a specific disorder, but their skill deficits are significant enough to cause them daily challenges and struggles. A large part of the challenge for these children is that we expect them to already have these skills. We place them in an age-based classroom and expect them to behave at a certain age-based level. For example, a child who is in Grade 4 and struggles to calm himself down when he gets angry is exhibiting behavior that is out of place for his age but would not raise concern in a Kindergarten class. We need to begin to understand the behavior of children in terms of a developmental skill deficit, for which the skill needs to be identified, taught, nurtured, and supported.

Physical Skills

Physical development is often separated into gross motor movements (crawling, reaching, sitting, running) and fine motor development (cutting, writing, hand–eye coordination). It is important not to simply view these physical movements in terms of a child's ability or the lack of ability to perform a task like walking, jumping, or talking. Most children in a classroom are able to perform these tasks with ease, without conscious thought and direction, without mental stress. But for some children, this is not the case. Even once these children have learned a task, repeating it does not come easily. That is because the ability to perform the physical movement involves thinking about, planning, sequencing, and executing a new motor action. Even tasks the child has performed many times require a great deal of effort. A new and unfamiliar task requires of all children a high degree of motor planning: for some it happens without effort and concentration; for others, each thought-to-limb movement requires explicit effort and thought.

Children who struggle with physical movement appear awkward, mechanical, uncoordinated, or clumsy. They know how to walk, run, and talk, but maneuvering their body gracefully around other children in the class and navigating gym class is challenging for them and exhausts their brains. A deficit of physical skills has social impact: these children bang into friends in the classroom, step on other kids' toes, are the last to be picked for a team. The physical skills include

- Fine Motor Movement: the coordination of small muscle groups, including fingers, hands, arms, shoulders, and neck; also involves hand–eye coordination.
- Motor Planning: the ability to plan, organize, sequence, and execute unfamiliar motor activities.
- Adaptability: the ability to generalize previously learned movements or skills.
- Body Awareness: the ability to think about one's body's movements and one's body's impact on the environment.
- Attending to Others: the ability to be aware of others and to focus on them.
- Verbal Impulse Control: the ability to resist stating a thought or idea out loud and/or to monitor what one says.
- Self-Control: the ability to resist a temptation, urge, action, or impulse.
- Matching Movement: the ability to observe others and follow their movements and patterns of behavior.
- Alternating Movement: the ability to switch movements and activities in motion.
- Self-Regulation: the ability to match one's body's energy levels to the needs of the environment.
- Movement Control: the ability to start and stop in motion.

Jenny: Motor Planning

Jenny's movements are slow and deliberate. When students are asked to get up from their desks and come to the carpet, Jenny does not move. She sits at her desk as if she did not hear the instructions. The teacher must come to her and tap her shoulder, then point to the carpet for Jenny to look up, nod, and move with the others.

Neil: Self-Control

Neil hits and pushes other children when he is upset or angry. These actions are not consciously deliberate; he does not plan in advance to push. These are

---

inappropriate actions, but are not done with forethought and planning, but rather are Neil's reactions when he is dysregulated.

Marsha: Matching Movement

Marsha does not observe the movements of others and match her movements to theirs. On the playground, she does not follow what the other children are doing and then join in with them. She walks off on her own with her own game idea in mind, then tries to convince other people to join in her game.

Lee: Self-Regulation

Lee has a hard time modulating his energy level. He zooms around the room, moving from one activity to another. He moves quickly and excitedly, without a clear purpose and plan.

Language Skills

Social language refers to the verbal and nonverbal language used to express one's social needs. It goes beyond knowing words and the names of things, which is essential enough for effective social interactions; it is the ability to use verbal and nonverbal means to connect with social partners. For example, social language is using language to get something, ask for help, tell a story, or share ideas and feelings. It is the area of language function that involves knowing what to say, how to say it, and when to say it. It is not limited to words, but also occurs through the eyes, face, and gestures.

It can be difficult for parents or teachers to recognize a deficit in these skills. Children can have strong verbal skills and a great vocabulary, but not use language to interact with others. They can lack the understanding and ability to use nuances that are needed in social interactions. Rather than being seen as children who need help expressing what they want to communicate, these children are sometimes thought of as quiet, shy, and without much to say.

Children with language delays typically have significant social delays. It is not simply that they are not able to communicate and play with their peers; it is also that they lack a broad range of social-emotional skills, only one of which is oral language. These children are typically weak in many language skills that make up social engagement and interaction; for example, gestures, looking at people's faces, engaging in back-and-forth conversation, expressing thoughts and feelings. This makes their play on the playground challenging. They are not checking in with their peer(s) to see what message is being sent to them; they are not sending their own message back. They lack intentional communication with others. Language skills include:

- Receptive Memory: the ability to input information into memory (encode it), create a permanent record of the information (store it), and later retrieve it (recall it).
- Processing: the ability to input information and then transform it by associating it with previously acquired information; once the information is outputted, it has been changed and has contextual value.
- Mindful Listening: the ability to stay focused on information and stay in the moment with the speaker.
- Nonverbal Communication: messages sent through the body and face.

- Intentional Verbal Communication: the ability to use language to send a message.
- Expressive Communication: the ability to use language to give detailed information to another person.
- Perspective-Taking: the ability to see another person's point of view and to see that the other individual has his/her own set of ideas, knowledge, and beliefs.
- Verbal Expansion: the ability to add a thought, comment, or statement to what another person has said.
- Verbal Messaging: the ability to monitor nonverbal and verbal tone and signals in a conversation.
- Storytelling: the ability to put detailed story events into narrative order.

Jenny: Processing

When students are asked to clean up for the day, Jenny stays at her seat and does not move. The clear verbal direction to clean up requires multiple thinking steps and coordination of knowledge that Jenny is unable to do.

Neil: Verbal Messaging

Even when Neil is explaining to his friends how to play a game he likes, his tone increases in harshness as he becomes more focused and excited about his game idea.

Marsha: Storytelling

Though Marsha's language abilities seem very strong, especially around factual information and conveying her opinion, Marsha is unable to tell a social story or tell her parents about her day at school.

Lee: Nonverbal Communication

When talking, Lee does not look at his peers and speak to them; his body is in motion and he moves and looks while he talks. As a result, other children do not understand that Lee is speaking with them.

Social Skills

Daily social engagements and interactions build positive or negative relationships, the underlying issues in bullying. All children need to be supported and guided in moment-to-moment interactions that develop healthy relationships based on the skills they are missing. If we support children through challenging and misunderstood interactions, then we support children's capacity to develop healthy relationships.

Some children seem to make play with others look effortless and fun. Not only do they gravitate toward other children, but other children gravitate to them as well. Social competence and the ability to develop and maintain positive social relationships requires a range of social-emotional skills that includes referencing, imitation, reciprocity, and perspective-taking. But on an even more basic level, children need to be socially motivated and to want to engage with, look to, and follow a peer. All of these social-emotional skills and the natural motivation to play set up a child to be able to practice play repeatedly and to begin to learn by repetition the skills that make play successful. Children who lack these skills and the motivation to play repeatedly miss out on the experiences of playing, and therefore are unable to build social skills. As these children grow up, their skills fall more and more behind those of their peers, and they withdraw even more. Social skills include

- Joint Attention: the process of paying attention to the same thing at the same time as a social partner.
- Social Reciprocity: the back-and-forth and give-and-take of social interaction.

- Social Imitation: the ability and motivation to look to another to copy his/her gestures, movements, and actions.
- Social Referencing: the ability to look at another to engage with them socially.
- Social Observation: the ability to look at another and the social environment to take in information.
- Emotional Sharing: the ability to match one's mood to the mood of others and the demands of the situation.
- Social Anticipation: the ability to move one's body in reaction to the movements of others.
- Social Receiving: the ability to accept the needs and movements of others and then move along with them.
- Space Awareness: the ability to share space with others and to move in reaction and relation to them.
- Reflective Appraisal: the ability to self-monitor and be aware of one's own behavior and not the behavior of others.

Jenny: Social Imitation

In class, the teacher provides detailed praise for the child who is on task, sitting properly, and working well. Once that praise is given, most other students look to that peer and copy what he/she is doing. Jenny misses this simple imitation learning experience. She does not look to the peer who is on task and does not copy his/her movements and actions. So Jenny remains off task, to the frustration of those around her.

Neil: Reflective Appraisal

Neil is offended by the misbehavior of others and insists that the teacher reprimand and punish other children when they are not following the rules or when they say something inappropriate. He genuinely does not seem aware that he, too, engages in this type of behavior, and doesn't understand if he has contributed to the other child's misbehavior.

Marsha: Social Reciprocity

When Marsha speaks or plays with other children, it is not fluid, back-and-forth play. She dominates the play and controls the ideas, objects, and game choices.

Lee: Emotional Sharing

It is not that Lee is unaware of the emotions of others; he is, in fact, hyper-aware of them and is very bothered by the noise and actions of others. As a result, when another child is hurt, Lee's behavior might seem odd, mean, or attention-seeking, since it involves his own socially inappropriate reaction to the other child's distress.

Emotional Skills

Some children seem to be always smiling, laughing, and enjoying every aspect of the day, while others are ever on the periphery, upset about something, too scared to join in, or feeling sad and left out. It should not be assumed that the child who is always happy is a nicer child or that the parents are doing something right. Nor should it be assumed that the parents of the child who worries indulge those worries and overprotect their child, or that the child who is angry is exposed to harsh parents at home. Moods come from within, and are based on

Moods are psychological states with emotional, cognitive, and behavioral aspects. For example, anxiety is a generalized reaction to a threat caused by a cognitive overestimation of danger. In danger, humans are adaptively programmed to fight, flight, or freeze. Anxiety is the behavioral reaction (fight, flight, or freeze) in the absence of clear danger or a level of danger that matches the reaction. With anxiety, instead of protecting the child from danger, the adaptive behavioral responses begin to interfere with the child's good coping strategies (Wagner, 2008).

a complex interplay between the external environment (the trigger; e.g., a dog), neurophysiological predisposition (internal reaction; e.g., heart racing), cognitive interpretation (bias toward interpreting events positively or negatively; e.g., *My heart is beating and there is a big dog. I am going to be attacked and get hurt*). The fact is that mood regulation is hard for some children. It is important to understand that these children do not overreact deliberately.

We can help children gain more emotional control by supporting them as they think through a high-stress situation. Slowly, gently, and consistently expose the child to events that have been shown to provoke anxiety for the child. But do so by empowering the child with prior knowledge and strategies to cope with the anxiety. Ensure that it is an exposure in which the child is uneasy, but that he/she can realistically manage and overcome. Successful experiences are the key learning tool. Emotional skills include

- Expressing Emotion: the ability to understand how to communicate emotions to others.
- Internalizing Emotions: the ability to link the body's internal sensations with an emotional vocabulary.
- Externalizing Emotions: understanding that there is a connection between the way we feel and the way we act.
- Emotional Regulation: identifying, understanding, monitoring, and managing appropriate moods and emotions; to match one's mood appropriately, positively, and constructively to the demands of the situation or environment.
- Emotional Modulation: the ability to emotionally rate the seriousness of environmental triggers or problems and react accordingly.
- Modulation of Tone: the ability to manage emotional expression.
- Optimistic Thinking: recognition that we can positively influence our thinking, which will in turn change the way we feel and act.
- Positive Affect: understanding that we can positively influence the way other people feel.
- Emotional Agency: understanding that positive and negative behavior affects how people feel.
- Emotional Liability: understanding the emotional perspective of others.

Neil: Managing Emotional Extremes

Neil has large outbursts in response to little problems.

Marsha: Emotional Modulation

Marsha's rigid thinking creates rules and issues that are not shared by many people. Marsha's love of nature and desire to preserve it mean that she gets upset at her peers over actions most other children would not notice or care about.

Lee: Externalizing Emotions

When a new teacher is frustrated and upset by Lee's unmanageable behavior, Lee senses the negative emotion toward him. This causes him internal distress and results in his engaging in more and more inappropriate behavior, not out of malice, but because of his dysregulation.

Cognitive Skills

These skills are of significant importance in the school system, because the executive function's development have academic effects: e.g., memory, processing speed, attention, making connections, prioritizing. Educationally, there is a growing body of literature on these skills and how they influence academic success. This book will examine the executive function's social-emotional skills that influence social success.

This continuum also includes the metacognitive aspects of development; i.e., thinking about learning. Children need to think about engaging, interacting, playing, and learning. The more children become self-aware and aware of their interactions with others, the more they will think about themselves and the way they play and learn. Being aware of their social contribution can help them begin to modify their way of thinking and, in turn, their behavior. Cognitive skills include

- Attending: the ability to pay attention to and stay focused on a non-preferred task.
- Switching Modalities: the ability to attend to multiple sources of information and to alternate between them.
- Information Sequencing: the ability to look to, attend to, and process information in sequence.
- Seeing the Whole Picture: the ability to focus on one task while maintaining an awareness of the environment as a whole.
- Flexibility: the ability to adapt and alter what one thinks, needs, and wants in response to the needs of others.
- Symbolic Thinking: the ability to think of things in abstract, varied, and non-literal ways.
- Recognizing Character: understanding the attributes that make up a person's character.
- Social Cognition: self-awareness and awareness of others as it applies to social situation and qualities.
- Behavior Modulation: understanding which behaviors will lead to social success; the ability to alter and adjust behavior based on personal desire to socially successful behavior.
- Social Narration: the ability to explain and retell social events.

> ### Jenny: Recognizing Character
>
> If asked to describe the boy she was just playing with, Jenny might say that he had a red shirt and striped socks. She might be unable to state his name, describe a physical characteristic unique to him, or detail anything about him as a friend or play partner. This lack of awareness of the qualities that make peers good playmates makes it hard to develop friendships.
>
> ### Neil: Social Cognition
>
> Neil has neither an accurate perception of himself as a person nor one of others. He understands social events through his negative emotions and therefore misperceives events and actions as being against him.

As long as the educational focus is not on helping children learn to learn and helping children develop social-emotional skills, the child's lack of attention will always be seen only as a disruption of the curriculum lesson.

Marsha: Flexibility

Marsha is rigid in her thinking and her belief system. Once she has logically constructed a rule or way of thinking, it is very hard for her to shift out of it. Marsha believes that it hurts nature to pull grass out of the lawn: debating this issue with her, especially in the heat of an argument, will not change her mind.

Lee: Social Narration

After a fight on the playground, Lee struggles to retell what happened and who was involved.

Identifying Skills Deficits

Just as you assess academic skills with checklists, rubrics, and assessments in the classroom, you can use a checklist to get an overview of your students' social-emotional skills, using the survey on pages 33–38.

1. Read over the survey a few times, so that you are aware of the descriptions and start to have a sense of which students might fit into particular sections.
2. If you can, write down students' names in sections you know will apply to them even before observation. When you are confident with these notes, you can write the names in pen. Highlight a specific student's name in the same color so that you can see at a glance how a student's skills cluster in particular domains.
3. Pencil in the names of other students for whom you believe the statements to be true, but might be unsure of.

If you color code the names of your students on the survey, you will be able to tell at a glance what group of skills each student has the most problems with.

This will give you a snapshot of the class as a whole, a picture that points to the skill deficits that need to be addressed the most by your particular class. This will point to which Active Skill Development games you can use with the whole class or groups of students. The point of the games is to explicitly teach and work on specific skills and for children to enjoy time together as a group. Focus on one skill area at a time, based on what you see as the greatest needs of your class as well as what you think you will be most comfortable introducing. Begin by choosing a game you think applies to the greatest issues for your class. The Active Skill Development games can be done repeatedly to help develop skills. These games are excellent just before lunch or at the end of the day. They can be brought into the daily schedule and played in centres as part of a daily social-emotional program.

See page 26 for more on Active Skill Development; page 29 for more on Moment-to-Moment Support.

The filled-in survey will also identify specific students with specific skills deficits, where Moment-to-Moment Support can be applied. The Moment-to-Moment strategies are specific to the skills of the section, but do not apply only to the games. They can be used throughout the day in class and on the playground. It is the consistent and daily use of these strategies with the children who struggle with the skill where real social growth takes place.

For example, a teacher would know that Jenny's behavior falls primarily into the Physical Skills section, Lee's into Social and Language Skills, Neil's into Emotional Skills, and Marsha's into Cognitive Skills. The teacher would write each name in the sections and then would mark the names beside the specific statements even before observational tracking.

Jenny

It becomes clear that Jenny is behind in the physical domain. She is unable to quickly adjust for and process slight changes in the environment; this results in a constant stress on her body and mind to focus on simple movements that most children take for granted. She has trouble combining and adjusting movements to fit changes in the environment: when a student moved a desk, it was hard for Jenny to walk around it; her mom indicated that when Jenny encountered a new climbing set it seemed like she had never used a climbing set before.

Neil

Neil's dominant challenge is in emotional skills. He could benefit from a program that helps him better understand his own emotions and his reactions when he is emotional, and can provide him with an increased awareness of the emotional experiences of others.

Marsha

Marsha struggles socially, but these struggles seem to stem primarily from her anxiety (emotional skills deficit) and her thinking (cognitive skills deficit).

Lee

Lee's social challenges result from his body's dysregulation in social situations, which causes him to move quickly and either speak too much or not enough.

Active Skill Development

In special education, students simultaneously receive remedial support as well as in-class accommodation. To return to our example of reading, a child who struggles with reading is pulled from class and taught to read through a reading intervention program. Tutoring, special education support, and extra reading work at home are ways that a student receives remedial support for reading. Simultaneously, teachers are expected to accommodate for that student in class; a student is not penalized in class for not being able to answer a question he or she cannot read.

We need to provide the same kind of support for children socially. Active skill development is the explicit teaching and building of a weak social-emotional skill. Most children need to be taught, for example, how to calm themselves down, how to slow down their breathing, and how understand the size and severity of a problem. Some children are taught this skill by their parents as toddlers, then it is reinforced for them in the preschool years, so that by the time they are in Grade 4 most of them do not need to be constantly reminded and supported in order to help calm themselves down. They no longer need this skill to be explicitly taught to them and they don't need to practice.

The games in this book are the explicit teaching. They outline and explain the specific skill deficits identified by looking at the behavior of the class, and are specifically designed to introduce a social-emotional skill and provide activity that supports that skill. They can be used with a whole class, or with homogenous groupings as extracurricular activities: e.g., for friendship clubs, or provided to a parent as a homework activity. Special education classes with multiple children with the same social-emotional skill deficits might pick one or two games at a time and play them as a warm-up in order to begin to teach the skill.

The expectation is not that the classroom teacher will seek out the skill deficit of a child and then repeatedly do a particular game in class to teach the skill. This would not be practical. The role of the classroom teacher is to use the process outlined in this book to begin to form a better understanding of the class, and of the social-emotional skill deficits that impede the learning of some students. The games can be used to support the weak skills in the classroom. They complement the drama, phys-ed, and language curriculum, and some of them are also simply fun games to play with the class as movement breaks.

Skill-Based Games

These games are not age-based; they are skill-based. It is indicated which games are appropriate for younger or older children; however, if an older child is weak in the particular skill, a game for older children might be too hard for that child, even if it is appropriate for the rest of the class. This problem is the very reason why these children are never able to improve their weak skills. As they grow up, their skills are a few grades behind those of their peers, but all the social learning they are doing is too hard for them. They are never learning the social skills at their own level, because it is assumed that, at their age, they should be able to perform these tasks.

There are many creative ways you can address this challenge. Many of the activities include explanations of how you can use social architecture (children with varying strengths that complement each other) to create internal scaffolding, in which the group is stronger than the sum of its parts and students can work together to individually gain skills (Peplar, 2006). Many of the activities can be done in homogenous groups or ability groups. The game chosen will be based on the peer group; i.e., if the teacher creates groups of children whose skill level is the same, then the activity will be at the correct level for every child in that group.

If the activity is not possible for the whole class or group, because the level of one child is so far behind that of the other children, then playing the game draws attention to what that child can't do and provides no learning. In this case, it is important to come up with ways to practice these games outside of the regular classroom, for example:

- Student teachers or educational assistants can provide opportunities to support a child on his/her own or with one or two other children with similar abilities, drawn from the classroom or the whole school.
- Bring the student to a class at a lower grade as a leader to help the younger children learn a skill. This experience builds the self-esteem of the older child while working on the weak skill. Instead of consistently sending a child to the office when his/her behavior disrupts the class, proactively provide breaks for the child to engage in some of the movement games with younger classes.

Though social-emotional skills should never be considered age-based, as they are developmental skills, I have included broad grade suggestions for the games. These grade suggestions indicate the class level for which you could use the game, as well as the grade by which the social-emotional skill is generally acquired. So, by the lower grade, most students would be expected to know and be able to perform the skill. For example, if the skill is generally acquired in Grade 4, the range of Grades 4 to 6 would emphasize that you want to support those students in Grades 5 and 6 who are somewhat behind the average in terms of the skill development.

Teach/Practice/Survive

The distinction between teaching (remediation) and guiding (accommodations and support) is important, as is understanding the appropriate times to do both. Teaching a child is introducing a concept, explaining it, giving examples, and listing information around it: e.g., teaching the concept of sharing would be to explain to a child what sharing is, why we do it, how we do it, when we do it. Moment-to-moment guiding of a child helps them perform something they already know about and understand; e.g., guiding a child would be to reinforce and encourage him/her to share a toy, a concept he/she already knows and understands but is not performing in the moment-to-moment interaction.

We often make the mistake of doing all our teaching and instruction while the child is performing the task, in the stressful situation. Just as the child is not sharing, we begin to teach the child about sharing, saying, "You need to share your toy. Sharing is an important aspect of being a friend and, if you don't share your toys, other children will not want to play with you." During the high-stress situation, this is too much information, too much direction, and too much lecturing.

Lee

When Lee's peers were taught the skills of having a conversation in Kindergarten, the lesson was developmentally appropriate for them, because their level of Social Reciprocity was at a stage where they were ready and able to apply it. When he was taught it alongside his peers, Lee was not ready to take in the teaching. The step-by-step instructions for a social conversation will need to be explicitly taught to Lee in Kindergarten, like all the other children. Then he will need it re-taught in Grades 1, 2, and 3.

Critics of intervention programs point out that the programs don't work because the child learns a skill in one environment and is unable to generalize the skill to another, more difficult, environment. If a child is being supported by an intervention program, it will work only if parents and teacher can help the child in the application of the skills he/she has learned. For example, if a child sees an occupational therapist, the more information you and the child's parents can gain from that program the better. You need to know what he/she is learning in these programs to support him/her.

Stress Level: Low

Building the social-emotional skills will not happen overnight. After being taught a base skill, the child needs to practice the skill repeatedly. So if we pinpoint a skill a child needs to build, the practice for this skill takes place in real life, in the moment, in the day-to-day social exchanges. This is moment-to-moment learning—the key point, where every teacher has the power to help a child apply a skill being learned, support the child in the practice of that skill, and guide the child by scaffolding the support systems, so that in each moment a child can be more successful socially.

A child needs to be able to learn a skill in a calm and systematic way—this is the teaching phase. Then the child needs repeated experiences with practicing that skill in many different environments—this is the practice phase. The child also needs a skilled advocate who understands that, in some environments or in states of high stress, the child will not be able to perform a skill he/she is able to do when he/she is regulated—this is the survive phase.

Teach/Active Skill Development

Children need to be taught social-emotional skills in a low-stress environment. They need the skill explained to them and they need multiple explicit teaching experiences in order to begin to build the skill. Ideally, this would be taught as an in-class lesson for the whole class, as part of in-school friendship and recess programs, and/or one-on-one by a parent, student teacher, or educational assistant.

Practice/Moment-to-Moment Support

Stress Level: Medium

Children need to be able to practice skills that are challenging for them in medium-stress environments. The child needs repeated exposure with supportive help from teachers or peers in order to practice and be successful in that skill with moment-to-moment support. This is the drill-and-repeat of social learning, and can be performed by the individual teacher, special-needs assistant, student teacher, and, most importantly, classroom peers to help a child have repeated successful practice in developing a weak social-emotional skill.

Survive/Meltdown and Crisis Response

Stress Level: High

Some children are unable to cope with high-stress environments. They become overwhelmed and hit a crisis point. In these high-stress situations, survival is the priority and calming down the child should be the teacher's only goal. When a meltdown is imminent, a teacher should stop focusing on the skill or task and help the child calm down. Moment-to-moment support during a meltdown switches from supporting the task or activity to supporting the child's regulation.

The process of identifying challenges, practicing them in real-life settings, and then slowly increasing levels of difficulty requires one or more dedicated adults to help create social learning opportunities over time.

Lee

Let's follow Lee through a few scenarios, starting in a recess friendship club in a classroom (easy environment), with an easy peer (who is flexible), and an easy activity (a structured game). This environment would be a Teach moment, a chance to introduce and teach skills to the children. Now let's go outside (difficult environment) for Ball Toss (easy activity) with an easy play peer (who follows and is quiet). This would be an excellent Practice opportunity for Lee. Finally, let's go inside to a large, open gym (medium-stress environment) for interactive activities (medium-stress activities) with a challenging peer (a leader and big talker). This combination will result in a high-stress scenario. This activity might be very stressful for Lee, so his behaviors might be challenging. An adult's focus in this final situation would be on regulating the environment and keeping him calm.

Moment-to-Moment Support

If a teacher reads this book and never once does any of these activities with students, even for fun, he/she can still apply the learning opportunities of the games to his/her teaching practice. The games establish a basis for work with individual students and show teachers how to target a skill, but might not be necessary in every situation. Each game demonstrates a skill deficit, the implications of these deficits, and ways to address this deficit in the moment; the last of these can be done with or without the game itself.

The moment-to-moment support will become the teacher's best teaching tool to help support the building of social-emotional skills with students. This support happens every minute of the day. It happens first thing in the morning as the children line up and it runs through every social interaction and teaching interaction. The moment-to-moment support happens along with and in the context of the games, but it also happens during all teaching moments. Moment-to-moment teaching uses daily interactions to show, model, explain, and problem-solve the thinking and feeling that goes into social interactions.

Moment-to-Moment Strategies

Each skill section includes suggestions for work with individual students in skill-building. Some of the moment-to-moment strategies apply directly to the game itself and others to academic or recess support, and some are home strategies for parents.

Chase the Skill

Create opportunities for children to practice their social-emotional skills: engage with them, let them speak, let them do the task, pushing them to use the skills you are helping them develop.

Detailed Positive Praise

Detail, in explicit language, the exact thinking, actions, and behavior that are helping the child be successful at school.

Grouping

Teachers can proactively choose what type of grouping (whole class, heterogenous, or homogenous) to use. You can specifically select children to increase success by using social architecture, creating groups based on promoting positive social interactions, and decreasing dynamics that trigger negative moment-to-moment interactions.

Homework

Be creative with homework and consider what is best for children in their overall development. Consider what skills a child needs and develop a basic homework plan around those skills. Photocopy the game and give it to the parents of the child to do nightly.

This is a much more effective way to communicate with a child's parents about a behavior that concerns you than summarizing or complaining about the child's challenging behavior.

Model

There will be more social success in a classroom where the teacher models acceptance, tolerance, empathy, self-awareness, collaborative problem-solving, and social thinking than in a teacher-dominated classroom where the rules are told to the children and apply only to them.

Nonverbal Cues

Without using words, show the child what to do with his/her body. Do not interrupt the activity or social interaction, simply gesture or point as a cue to help the child better succeed at a task.

Be sure to cue as much as the child needs in order to be successful, but as little as possible, so that the child is not dependent on you.

Paraphrase

Instead of labeling a child's statement as inappropriate, rephrase the statement for the child in a way that is socially productive. Do not tell the child to say it or use the word "say"; simply repeat the sentence you want the child to say.

Peer Facilitation

Prompt children to interact and communicate instead of using just adult-to-child engagement. Support their interaction without taking it over, interrupting, or making eye contact (i.e., look down to allow students to make eye contact with each other).

Peer Scaffolding

This is the process through which a peer assists a learner so that the learner can achieve beyond his/her own ability.

Praise the Learning Process

Instead of rewarding the final accomplishment or the end product, focus on giving feedback and praise on the learning process itself. This creates learners who are aware of the skills it took them to accomplish the task, instead of children who are proud of themselves only for doing it right, or who tried hard but did not succeed in the final task and are unmotivated to try again.

Proactive Explanation

Warn and give detailed description of what is coming next and the explicit explanation of the expected behavior to prepare the student in advance and decrease disruptive behavior.

Redo

Allow children to go back to a starting point and redo an activity in order to make a better choice.

Regulate the Environment

The pace of the environment can make a child very excited or disengaged. You can tweak aspects of the pace of the environment to help the child's body calm down or become more alert. You can modify the speed of the activity by stopping, pausing, slowing down, changing the volume and intonation of your voice.

Reward Systems

Token systems or small, easily earned points are most effective. Make the tasks small, manageable, and unconditional and then provide the reward as soon as possible.

Well-created reward systems can help children focus on their behavior, and can motivate them to self-monitor and alter their behavior while skill-building. Reward systems should be individualized and should aim to reward each child multiple times a day for whatever that child is working on.

Scaffolding

Provide help so the child can successfully accomplish a task he/she could not do on his or her own. With support, children can experience greater success on tasks and then eventually learn the skills to do them without the support.

Self-Talk

Instead of telling what the child should be thinking and doing, and how the child should be modifying his/her behavior, show the child the skills through your own thinking.

Structure

If the children have been involved in creating the classroom systems, labeling (drawing the visuals), and placing elements in the room (at their height), then they gain ownership of the room. Every child in the room should be able to access their materials and the resources of the class independently and they should know how to navigate the room, task by task, on their own or with the help of their peers.

Understanding the Skill Deficit

Understand that the child can do the task, but that it takes that child more time, energy, or support to do it.

Verbal Cues

Using words, explain to the child exactly what to do with his/her body, his/her actions, and his/her words. These directives should be as simple and detailed as possible and should set the child's interaction up for success, but should not be judgments on behavior.

Verbal Thinking Cues

Explain or cue the thoughts that would help the child in his/her decision-making process in the task.

Zone of Proximal Development

When we test children, we want them to show us what they know; we should therefore test with leveled materials within their proficiency. During the school day, if we want children to grow and learn, we should be providing material just outside that level of proficiency; i.e., in their zone of proximal development (Vygotsky, 1986). This means exposing them to tasks that involve some sort of outside support, tasks that truly challenge the child and force him/her to stop, consider options, and seek some amount of assistance before being able to perform a skill he/she cannot do on his/her own.

Class Survey

Type of Skill	Skill	Signs of Skill Deficit	Student(s)															
Physical	Fine Motor Movement	Poor posture and weak body movements																
		Poor hand–eye coordination																
		Poor bodily coordination																
	Motor Planning	Movements slow, jerky, mechanical, rigid																
		Is overwhelmed or exhausted after new tasks																
	Adaptability	Difficulty learning new movements																
		Always moves in the same way																
		Unable to generalize previously learned movements																
	Body Awareness	Moves quickly and heavily																
		Bangs into things and people																
	Attending to Others	Seems unaware of the presence of others																
		Does not react to verbal statements or movement of others																
	Verbal Impulse Control	Interjects statements while someone is talking																
		Interrupts discussions with irrelevant information																
	Self-Control	Moves quickly without thinking																
		Acts before considering consequences																
	Matching Movement	Fails to match the movement of environment or others																
		Is out of sync with the speed and movement of others																
	Alternating Movement	Struggles with transitions																
		Has difficulty stopping preferred activities																
		Has difficulty alternating or switching movements																
	Self-Regulation	The body and energy level do not match the situation or environment																
		Has a hard time identifying his/her body's energy level																

© 2013 *Moment by Moment* by Joey Mandel. Pembroke Publishers. ISBN 978-1-55138-287-6.

Class Survey (continued)

Type of Skill	Skill	Signs of Skill Deficit	Student(s)
	Self-Regulation	Does not connect his/her influence over physical behavior with ability to manage his/her own regulation	
		Lacks sensory tools to calm down or be ready to learn	
	Movement Control	Unable to start and stop in motion on his/her own	
		Has difficulty starting and stopping in motion in response to a request	
Language	Receptive Memory	Does not move after instruction	
		Unable to receive and recognize auditory or visual information	
	Processing	Unable to complete tasks that involve inferences	
		Unable to sort out information within a task	
		When faced with a challenge, does not take active steps to get help	
	Mindful Listening	Unable to demonstrate understanding using verbal communication	
		Does not follow verbal instruction	
	Nonverbal Communication	Does not look to others to send information	
		Does not attempt to convey a message through gestures, facial expression	
	Intentional Verbal Communication	Struggles to use words to explain him/herself	
		Unable to form sentences to explain him/herself	
	Expressive Communication	Does not use language to provide information to another	
		Does not use language to send a message	
	Perspective-Taking	Does not ask questions to find out about another	
		Does not understand that conversations are two people talking back and forth	
	Verbal Expansion	Does not add to what another says	
		Contradicts what another says	

© 2013 *Moment by Moment* by Joey Mandel. Pembroke Publishers. ISBN 978-1-55138-287-6.

Class Survey (continued)

Type of Skill	Skill	Signs of Skill Deficit	Student(s)
	Verbal Messaging	Uses a harsh tone and words when disagreeing with the group	
		Uses a rude tone and expressions when others do not agree with him/her	
	Storytelling	Struggles to tell a story verbally	
		Unable to tell a story with a beginning, middle, and end	
		Has difficulty writing a story	
		Has difficulty with a non-preferred story starter	
Social	Joint Attention	Is more interested in toys and objects than in other children	
		Has less motivation to play with a peer than to play with a toy	
	Social Reciprocity	Moves, plays, and talks in his/her own world with no back and forth with other children	
		Plays on his/her own without giving, showing, handing, or looking to peers	
	Imitation	Does not look to and copy the movements of others	
		Does not move with and react to the movements of others	
	Referencing	Unable to speak with someone while looking that person in the eyes	
		Looks away from person he/she is speaking to	
	Social Observation	Does not look around to get information about what other children are doing or feeling	
		Does not observe the reactions or gestures of other children	
	Emotional Sharing	Does not notice or react to the emotions or needs of others	
		Hyper-reacts to the moods of others	
	Social Anticipation	Has difficulty appreciating the impact of his/her behavior on another	
		Does not anticipate the movements of others or understand that their movements will influence him/her	

Class Survey (continued)

Type of Skill	Skill	Signs of Skill Deficit	Student(s)
	Social Receiving	Does not consider the point of view of another	
	Space Awareness	Unable to accept or see what another person needs	
		Moves too close into another's space	
		Discloses too much information	
	Reflective Appraisal	Is aware of the misbehaviors of others	
		Lacks the perspective that rules are for him/her too	
Emotional	Expressing Emotion	Unaware of how he/she reacts to his/her own emotions	
		Has an inflated emotional reaction without understanding what it looks like to others	
	Internalizing Emotions	Does not understand the different physical sensations that emotions create in the body	
		Confuses one emotion for another	
	Externalizing Emotions	Unable to link positive or negative emotions to physical sensations and his/her reactionary behavior	
		Does not understand that behavioral reactions are not socially acceptable	
	Emotional Regulation	Reacts in the moment to extreme negative feelings	
		Gets very upset and is unable to calm down	
		Is not aware that the tools used to calm our bodies when energized can be used when we are upset	
	Emotional Modulation	Reacts to small problems in big ways	
		Has extreme reactions to problems	
		View of what is a big problem differs from that of most people	
	Modulation of Tone	Expresses negative emotions when speaking with others	
		Negative emotion is expressed verbally	

© 2013 *Moment by Moment* by Joey Mandel. Pembroke Publishers. ISBN 978-1-55138-287-6.

Class Survey (continued)

Type of Skill	Skill	Signs of Skill Deficit	Student(s)
	Optimistic Thinking	Interprets every situation in a negative way	
		Thinks about a situation from a negative viewpoint	
	Positive Affect	Does not understand that his/her moods can change the moods of others	
		Does not connect his/her positive behaviors and the moods of others	
	Emotional Agency	Does not make the connection between behavior and how he/she feels	
		Does not understand that actions have emotional impact on him/herself and others	
	Emotional Liability	Does not understand that others have challenges and struggles too	
		Cannot see the emotional perspective of others	
Cognitive	Attending	Does not pay attention to what others want him/her to pay attention to	
		Does not stay on task; is easily distracted	
	Switching Modalities	Starts a task but does not complete it	
		Requires sustained, one-dimensional effort to engage in tasks	
		Has a hard time with tasks that require two skills or switching from one skill to another	
	Information Sequencing	Does not accurately visually process information	
		Does not attend visually or look around to observe the environment	
	Seeing the Whole Picture	Notices little details in the room or about people, but misses attending to the lesson, the game, or what another is saying	
		Misses the underlying point, idea, or concepts	

Class Survey (continued)

Type of Skill	Skill	Signs of Skill Deficit	Student(s)
	Flexibility	Gets stuck on one idea or outcome	
		Tries the same solution or expresses the same thought repeatedly, even if it does not work and is not accepted by others	
	Symbolic Thinking	Struggles with shifting his/her thinking and with attempting a new strategy	
		Is literal in his/her interpretation of the world and language	
		Does not engage in creative and imaginary play	
	Recognizing Character	Describes and identifies others with a single physical or action description, instead of what they are like as people	
	Social Cognition	Is unaware of him/herself and his/her own character qualities	
		Is unaware of the impact of his/her character on others	
	Behavior Modulation	Does not understand how to behave in given social situations	
		Does not understand which behaviors lead to positive and negative social success	
	Social Narration	Unable to explain or share social events	
		Cannot transfer information from one setting to another	

2

Actively Developing Physical Skills

Fine Motor Movement

Looking Beyond the Behavior

In a student with weak fine motor skills, you will observe
- difficulty with precision using fingers and hands
- weak body movements
- poor posture
- poor hand–eye coordination

Understanding Fine Motor Skills

In school, fine motor skills are looked at when a child exhibits messy handwriting and the inability to draw or to cut. The lack of development of the small muscles involved in writing might be caused not only in the fingers and hands, but also in the whole arm and the neck. This could affect the child's posture and result in the child leaning in on his/her hands and slouching down too close to his/her work. This awkward body posture has social repercussions, as the child seems disengaged during group work. If we help children practice activities that require movements of the fingers, wrists, elbows, shoulders, neck, trunk, and upper extremities, we can help them develop muscle strength, joint stability, dexterity, and hand–eye coordination; this will not only help in printing, but also will help them play with toys at the carpet and participate in sports with their friends on the playground.

Active Skill Development

- to build the coordination of small muscle groups, including fingers, hands, arms, shoulders, and neck
- to build hand–eye coordination

Human Jenga

Instructions

Grades K–3
Approximate Time: 15 minutes

1. Place pails full of small balls around the room.
2. Create a series of hurdles or obstacles: e.g., rope strung just above the ground; benches they have to step over; swimming noodles; blocks or empty cereal

boxes piled so they are hard to step over without having them crash down; balls placed on the tops of pails that fall off if touched. You can use bowling pins as an extra obstacle.

3. Have students line up at one end of the room in two groups. Tell students they will be throwing the balls at the walls on their own side, trying not to hit each other with them. Instruct them to grab the ball and demonstrate how to throw at targets you have taped to the wall at various heights:
   - Throw high: extend arm fully up in the air and throw
   - Push pass: bend from the elbow and pass in front
   - Grounder: bend the body from the knees and roll the ball

4. At your signal, the first students from each group will begin to move across the gym through the obstacle course. Each time the student passes a pail, he/she must pick a ball and throw it using one of the three throws.

5. This is not a race between the groups, so the next student in the group can start when the first child finishes with the first ball throw. Or you can monitor the movement and signal when you think that the next team member can go without catching up to the student in front of him/her.

Grabbing a ball is an excellent way to strengthen the muscles used in a pencil grip.

Discussion Before and After

- Discuss what other activities students could apply the same movements to.
- Reflect on how hard it was to avoid the obstacles while focusing on throwing the balls.

Moment-to-Moment Support

Grouping

You have two choices for your groupings.
- Mixed-ability grouping for children who work well together. Be careful that this activity not turn into a race.
- Ability grouping, with different obstacles set up for each course, based on the capabilities of the group. The advantage of this is that each child can work on an obstacle course at his/her own level.

Zone of Proximal Development

In all activities, we want our students to be successful. Start off with larger, more-durable objects, like big boxes. Slowly increase the number of small and fragile objects.

Peer Scaffolding

Once students have mastered this activity, add steps that create social engagement and help them practice peer interactions that will be used at other times: e.g., have them turn to peers and list back the steps of the obstacle course, then ask a peer to repeat the obstacle course in reverse order.

Self-Talk

This strategy can be used any time, not just with the game. "This part coming up is a little tricky. I think I am going to slow down and look first. I am going to think first and move my feet slowly, one step at a time."

Chase the Skill

Take the focus off of pencil grip and fine motor coordination during writing itself, so that a child with weak fine motor skills does not become frustrated with the writing and reading process. Build the skill at separate times; pointing your finger, finger-painting, ball tosses, rice counting, money sorting, finger-puppet shows, and arm aerobic exercises all build fine motor control without associating it with a pencil.

Homework

Send home a description of the activity. Include these instructions:

> Encourage your child to make obstacle courses with you. Be sure that he/she contributes some ideas but that you do too. While going through the obstacle course, be sure to help your child talk out loud and list each step: for example, "First we go under the rope, then we step over the bench."

Motor Planning

Looking Beyond the Behavior

In a student with weak motor planning skills, you will observe
- movements are slow, jerky, mechanical, and rigid
- the child is overwhelmed or exhausted after new tasks
- the child appears to take great effort to bend down to pick up something off the floor

Understanding Motor Planning Skills

Motor planning is the ability to plan, organize, sequence, and execute unfamiliar motor activities. For any action or task (e.g., reach out and hold on to the rope of a swing), one needs to examine the object, see where it is in the physical space, plan the body's movement toward the object, and relay messages throughout the body to coordinate the movements it will require to perform the task (reach out and grab the rope). We can help children internally sequence their movements through rhythm, beat, and recurrent motions.

Active Skill Development

- to build the ability to plan, organize, sequence, and execute unfamiliar motor activities

Merry-Go-Round

Instructions

Grades K–3
Approximate Time: 30 minutes

1. Set up circuits, using hoops, ropes, inclines, cones, benches, mats, etc.
2. Use tape or a line to let students know where they should stand while waiting.

3. Tell students where the child in front of them should be before they start their turn.
4. Give students specific instructions for what they do at the end of the circuit; i.e., line up behind the last child and be ready to go again.
5. Each student should perform the circuit five times before it is modified or added to.

Discussion Before and After

- Discuss where your eyes are looking during the different stages of the circuit.
- Reflect on the different movements your body performs during the circuit.

Moment-to-Moment Support

Grouping

Have children work in small homogenous groups; i.e., group students for each circuit based on ability, so you can slightly modify each circuit. Since abilities vary between groups, the speed of each circuit will be different, and children who want to go fast will not overwhelm children who need to go more slowly.

Zone of Proximal Development

Be sure to plan the circuit so that each student is working on obstacles "just right" for him/her. If you see a child struggling at a particular section, help him/her achieve success by giving your hand to provide a needed boost, by giving one extra stepping block to climb over something high, or by removing a step from that circuit.

Model

Demonstrate the obstacle course a few times so that children with weaker skills are able to see the movements multiple times. If you have different circuits, pick a few volunteers to demonstrate; use this while a student with a skill deficit is practicing the circuit, so that all students are not watching that student.

Self-Talk

Encourage each student to verbally state the steps out loud as he/she performs each action: "First, I am throwing the yellow ball into the bucket. Then I need to crawl through the tunnel."

Peer Scaffolding

If a child is unable to self-talk as he/she goes through the circuit, have a peer walk beside and state the steps out loud for the child, encouraging the child to participate.

Nonverbal Cues

If a student struggles to move when you give group instructions to the class, consider moving near the child and tapping his/her arm or pointing in a signal to indicate the first step required. For example, if you tell students to pick up their pencils and one student does not, consider moving his/her hand toward the pencil as the first action of the task.

Homework

Send home a description of the activity. Include this suggestion:

> Add rhythm to the movement. Use music, drums, counting, clapping, and tapping to beat out a pattern. Move with your child to match a sound to each movement.

Adaptability

Looking Beyond the Behavior

In a student with weak adaptability skills, you will observe
- difficulty learning new movements
- inability to generalize previously learned movements
- inability to apply different types of movement to different physical spaces

Understanding Adaptability Skills

Once a motor skill is mastered (e.g., hopping like a rabbit in a gym game), a child should be able to use the same motor movement for different physical activities. Some children are not able to apply the movement skills they learned for one task to another task. We can support these students by understanding that, just because they were able to perform it one day in one environment, we can't expect them to easily reproduce the movement. We can also help them transfer what they have learned in one environment to another by helping them recall the steps it took them to learn it and apply those steps to another context.

Active Skill Development

- to build the ability to generalize previously learned movements or skills

Zig-Zag

Instructions

Grades K–3
Approximate Time: 15 minutes

You will need a large open space for this activity. You can post images of different movements on the wall.

1. Discuss with students the importance of looking out for each other and being aware of each other's space.
2. Students begin by walking according to the type of movement you call out: walk backwards, in straight lines, zig-zag, in waves, in swirls, in circles, etc.
3. Introduce new movements slowly. Signal to pause between movements. Have students freeze and close their eyes. Tell them you are going to call out the next movement, but that they cannot move for a count of five. During that time, they have to think about the movement and how they are going to perform it.
4. Introduce one new movement at a time, then go back and repeat movements that have already been learned.
5. When you feel that students have mastered a movement at a comfortable speed, slowly encourage them to walk "a little faster" then "even a little faster."

Discussion Before and After

- Discuss what students think about when they are preparing to do a movement.
- Reflect on how easy or hard it was to hear a verbal command and then alter the movement pattern.

Moment-to-Moment Support

Grouping

If you have identified a student whose movements are mechanical and rigid, pair up him/her with a students whose movements are not too quick and fast. Even at a desk for group work, the child with weak adaptability skills will be better able to keep up because of the slower speed of the other child's movements.

Regulate the Environment

See page 57 for more on self-regulation.

If one student begins to become dysregulated during this activity—e.g., starts acting silly, running too fast, moving uncontrollably—shadow that student physically instead of calling out his/her name. Verbal direction will not help this child slow down and focus. Move to the child, gently place your hand on his/her shoulder or give him/her something heavy to hold during the activity. The deep pressure of your touch or the heavy weight of an object are sensory tools that will help the student self-regulate.

Peer Support

This is an excellent opportunity to use older students who struggle with self-regulation for support. These older students develop empathy and their own physical movement control by leading and walking just in front of a younger child who is struggling to perform these movements.

Verbal Cues

"Well done. It is hard to focus on your own movement while predicting the movements of your friends and reacting to their movements." Say this during the game, but also at recess, around the school, and even in the classroom, so that children begin to understand different forms of large and small movements and their connection to the movements of others.

Zone of Proximal Development

It is important to focus on one skill at a time. If you are chasing behavior and skill-building, first consider the activity and the state of the child. Skill-build when the child is in a calm state. When the child is performing a task that is hard for him/her, simply support the child through a challenging task without adding more target skills.

Homework

Send home a description of the activity. Include this suggestion:

> Add gestures and actions to the movement. Once you have performed any sequence five or more times, begin to add extra body actions while moving: for example, "While we walk in zig-zag, we can shake our hips to the rhythm of the music. We can clap and count as we walk backward."

Body Awareness

Looking Beyond the Behavior

In a student with weak body awareness skills, you will observe
- the student moving quickly and heavily around the classroom
- the student banging into things and people
- the student running into desks, stepping on toes, and tripping over backpacks

Understanding Body Awareness Skills

Physical body control and movement awareness allow a child to navigate through and around objects and other children in his/her physical space. Children need to be aware of where their body starts and where it ends. Some children move quickly with large, loud, and quick gross motor responses. They have a poor sense of where their body is in space and how it moves in relation to the objects and people around it. For example, a child with poor body awareness is not aware of exactly how to move his/her arm and bring it up to his/her face to put a straw in his/her mouth. As a result, these children tend to be messy eaters, as they are unable to coordinate the movements required to accurately feed themselves. If children struggle with this skill, it should not be surprising that they also struggle, for example, to avoid banging into the chair as another child pulls a seat back.

Active Skill Development

- to develop the ability to think about his/her body's movements and his/her body's impact on the environment

Got Ya

Instructions

Grades K–6
Approximate Time: 15–30 minutes

1. Have one or two students stand in the middle of the room with their eyes closed. They are the Detectives.
2. Instruct everyone else to spread out around the Detectives.
3. Students move around without the Detectives hearing them. They can come as close to or go as far away from the Detectives as they want, but must be slow, quiet, and deliberate in their movements, so as not to be heard.
4. When a Detective hears a noise, he/she can open his eyes, look at and/or point at the moving child, and say, "Got ya!" with a smile on his/her face and

in a kind and gentle tone. The child who was heard moving goes right back into the game.

5. No one is Out in this game. Use it as an opportunity to teach the pleasure of games in and of themselves, not for winning and losing.

Discussion Before and After

- Discuss what students need to do in order not to be heard by the Detective.
- Reflect on the fact that, as they got excited and worked hard to control their movements, their breathing increased and their heart rates went up.

Moment-to-Moment Support

Scaffolding

Remember, the student who needs to work on this activity the most is the one who will be caught most often. Let him/her play and let him/her practice. Support that student by placing him/her at the back of the room, furthest from the Detective. Place students who are slow and deliberate in their movements (i.e., who have strong body awareness skills) close to the Detective at the front.

Detailed Positive Praise

Be sure to give positive detailed praise explaining the actions that make the task successful. For example, "Well done, Lee. You took a deep breath before you started moving. This calmed and relaxed your whole body. I see that you are slowly moving one leg at a time."

Regulate the Environment

In order to help children be more mindful of their bodies and movement, slow students down before you begin any activity. When you have children sit at circle or at their desks, consider doing one long-breathing, full-body stretch, ideally incorporating a balancing pose (the Tree pose for yoga is an excellent one) to centre the children and focus their attention on their bodies and their breathing.

Chase the Skill

Incorporate thinking about one's body movement into all activities of the day. As you walk with your class, tell the children to slow down or be quick, or walk to avoid detection from the students in the other classes and the other teachers in the hall.

Homework

Send home a description of the activity. Include this suggestion:

> You can try this activity wearing different clothes and on different surfaces. Often it is the clothes rustling or the movement of shoes that one is able to hear while playing this game. So to start, play this game with your child in his/her bathing suit on grass or a beach. It will be harder to hear your child's movements, so he/she will be more successful at the game. As your child practices and becomes stronger at the game, make it more challenging by wearing clothes that make more noise as they crinkle, wearing shoes, and playing on wooden floors that creak.

> ### Lee
> The space in the room is defined, using color and sectioning. Colored tape is put on the floor to make paths; there are carpeted areas and areas with mats. Furniture and objects in the class are removed to open the space and simplify it.

Attending to Others

Looking Beyond the Behavior

In a student with poor skills in attending to others, you will observe
- the student seems unaware of the presence of others
- the student does not react to verbal statements or movement of others

Understanding the Skills of Attending to Others

Children who are aware of the presence of others are successful in play because they are able to react to and respond to the movements, statements, and emotions of their friends. This increases the chances of successful social interactions. It is important to consistently draw children's attention to the other people with whom they share space, not only with their eyes, but with their ears too.

> ### Jenny
> If Jenny is working at a table and does not notice another child come into the area, not stopping, looking up, or saying hello, Jenny will appear rude. Before Jenny can look up and say hello, she needs to be more attuned to the movements and sounds of others, so that she notices them come into her space.

Active Skill Development

- to build the ability to be aware of other people and to focus on them

Stealth

Instructions

Grades K–3
Approximate Time: 15 minutes

1. All students sit on the ground, on a carpet, or at their desks.
2. One child, the Listener, sits on a chair with his/her back to the class. The chair should be a good distance from the rest of the group.
3. An object is placed under the chair.
4. Pick another child to be Stealth. Stealth tries to go into the Listener's space and quietly take the object without being heard.

Discussion Before and After

- Discuss how much effort it takes for Stealth to control his/her body, to move slowly and quietly.
- Reflect on how hard each child found it to share space. Did they enter other people's space? Were their actions covert and stealthy or loud and energetic?

Moment-to-Moment Support

Nonverbal Cues

If a student has a hard time paying attention as Listener, gently place your hand on the child or object that the student is distracted by. If the student looks up at you, point and signal where he/she should be looking, i.e., at the person who just entered his/her space without getting his/her attention. Provide the student with a cue to smile and say hello to the person.

Chase the Skill

Being aware of other children, turning attention to others, and being present in the play can help lead to successful interaction. Children who move around quickly, leave play, and do not attend to their peers have a harder time building relationships and practicing play. Teach children what it actually looks like to sit and play with other children.

Detailed Positive Praise

Identify situations in which you see a quick-moving child doing something slowly with thought or precision. "Lee, that was amazing. You were about to bump into your friend, then you noticed her, slowed down, and moved around her. Well done."

Redo

Instead of disciplining a student for moving too fast or bumping into something or someone, use a redo. Simply walk up to the student, nod in an encouraging way, and say, "Let's try walking past your friend again more slowly so that you can move around his/her body." Then lead the student back to where he/she was before starting to move too fast and let him/her walk again, slowly, avoiding contact with the other student.

Model

"Oh wow, I thought I was working on my own here and I just looked up and saw that three people joined my group. I guess I was so focused on my book that I was unaware of what was going on around me. It is great to be focused on my work, but I need to stop and check in with the class every few minutes to make sure I am not missing anything." Follow this verbal statement with your nonverbal reaction. Show your surprise and your awareness of the movements of other people. When someone joins a group, show your awareness of someone coming into the space and your acknowledgment of them. Give the newcomer a big nod and smile. Keep showing students what we do when someone enters the group.

Homework

Send home a description of the activity. Include this suggestion:

> When you play this game at home with your child, be sure to understand your role in the play. Too often, adults get so involved with the game they forget their support role. Your job in this game is to help your child learn skills. So when your child sits in the chair and you are Stealth, make sure you are not exceptionally quiet. You can show your child what *not* to do: slap your hands against the floor; smash your feet to the ground. Let your child catch you right away and give a look of surprise that you got caught. Most likely your child will be able to tell you exactly what you need to do to be more quiet and not make noise. Continue your movement, talking out loud about how you need to try to bring your arm up slowly so you do not make noise; "I need to gently place my hand on the ground so it does not make noise." When you become the Listener, be sure not to turn around quickly and catch your child. Even if he/she is loud, give him/her time to practice the activity and to move slowly across the carpet. Catching your child only discourages him/her and results in a pause in the game.

Verbal Impulse Control

Looking Beyond the Behavior

In a student with weak verbal impulse control skills, you will observe
- the student interjects statements while someone is talking
- the student interrupts discussions with irrelevant information

Understanding Verbal Impulse Control Skills

We need to help children understand that verbal interruption is an impulsive act, then that they need to practice not adding to a conversation at an inappropriate time. Be careful not to be inconsistent with children who interrupt: sometimes, we tell them that they are interrupting; other times we take what they say and we react to it. This is based on the amount of time we have in the situation, the mood we are in, the value of what they say. However, we do not explain that to children. We need to help them distinguish between when they should and should not comment, between what they can comment on to help a conversation and what is unhelpful interrupting. This needs to be explicitly taught to them, with examples and situations. No matter how many children understand not to interrupt, they all need practice at holding in something they want to say. They need to be given time to practice and mental-distraction tools to use to prevent blurting out their thoughts.

Active Skill Development

- to practice the ability to resist stating a thought or idea out loud
- to monitor what one says

Hold Your Tongue

Grades K–3
Approximate Time: 15 minutes

Proactively bring this activity into everyday life. For example, before gym class, remind students of "our little Hold Your Tongue game."

Instructions

1. Explain that you are going to play a copy game: e.g., Karate Moves, Simon Says, Follow The Leader. The goal of the game is to copy the body's movements, to focus with the eyes, and to imitate. But the most important rule is that no one but the leader is allowed to talk.
2. Let students know before the game starts that you are going to talk about things that they want to talk about. Tell them, "But sometimes, like in class, during karate lessons, or when someone else is talking, we need to keep what we want to say inside our heads."
3. While you do simple moves for them to copy, talk out loud about things you know they want to add information to. For example, name a karate move after something a child would have a connection to and want to talk about: "This move is called the Monkey" might lead the child to say, "My grandma has a monkey."
4. Once they understand interruptions, add in the concept of correcting. For example, call moves by the wrong name. If necessary, use a chart to help students list what information is important to correct (i.e., when it will affect the message you are conveying) and statements that we do not need to correct (i.e., when everyone knows what the person means and it will not matter that information is missing).
5. Be sure to set time aside after the game to listen to the story and hear what they have to say. Reward them for telling you the story at the right time.

Discussion Before and After

- Discuss the difference between a conversation with a friend, when you can add to what your friend says, and situations in which someone is talking when you should not add to what they are saying.
- Reflect on a time you were trying to explain something and someone kept interrupting your story to add on to it.

Moment-to-Moment Support

Scaffolding

Gently place your hand on the child's shoulder if you can tell that the child is about to begin speaking or if the child already has.

Verbal Thinking Cues

"You can think about this game when you are in math class. If I am explaining a lesson and it reminds you of a great story, it might not be the time to tell it to the class. Even if you have a great thought or story to tell, you have to wait until after the class."

Nonverbal Cues

Be kind and encouraging. At the beginning, reward them with little smiles when they don't correct you. Then phase this out, because it is still signaling to them that you know what they wanted to say. Use the same nonverbal cues throughout the day when a student interrupts a lesson or another student. Look at the student, nod to acknowledge that you have seen him/her and can hear him/her, but continue your sentence to indicate that it is your turn to speak and that you will not stop mid-sentence when someone interrupts you.

Proactive Explanation

"What will you think about inside your head to prevent yourself from telling a story or saying something that you should not? It is not enough to tell yourself not to talk; you also need to distract your brain and think about something to help you not interrupt. You could even say inside your head, 'I will close my mouth and listen with my ears. It is not the time to tell my story.'"

Regulate the Environment

If a student interrupts and talks a lot, slow down the pace of the classroom or consider playing slow, quiet music. A calmer child will be more regulated and will therefore have more ability to use self-control.

Self-Talk

Model the internal dialogue you would like students to use. For example, while getting ready to go outside for recess, use the think-aloud process to show what the child should be doing. "Right now I am trying to get ready to go outside for recess. My brain is focused on all the things I need to do to get ready for recess. I am thinking about my list of things I need in order to be ready for recess: my snack, my coat, and my recess play plan. I am not thinking about telling a story or anything that does not have to do with recess."

Reward System

It is always easier to reinforce behavior that children do than to reward them for the omission of behavior. But it is important to catch a child who does not engage in the negative behavior you have been trying to help them decrease. You can reward a child who was just about to start a behavior but stopped him/herself; you can also reward a child who does not engage in a certain behavior in a set time period. For example: "Lee, I saw that you were just about to interrupt me, but then you stopped yourself" or "Lee, I was able to get through my whole lesson without you adding comments while I was talking. Thank you."

Homework

Send home a description of the activity. Include this suggestion:

> Once your child has mastered this game, you can apply it to any activity you do together. For example, you can play Hold Your Tongue while throwing a football or getting ready to go to school. Understand that the purpose of this game is not to take away fluid back-and-forth conversation with your child, which is a wonderful skill and something we want to encourage. This game is about teaching your child not to interrupt and tell a long story when he/she should be focusing on something or someone else.

Self-Control

Looking Beyond the Behavior

In a student with weak self-control skills, you will observe
- student acts before considering consequences
- student moves quickly without thinking
- student walks past a desk and pushes papers off it

Understanding Self-Control Skills

Some children move around the room quickly without having to think through what they will touch, where their bodies will go, or their movement plan. In order to gain greater control over their bodies' movements, other children need to strengthen the connection between their thinking brain and their moving body. They need to practice moving slowly and thinking before moving. We are quick to tell children to slow down, but it is much harder to support these quick-moving children. We often shy away from school and home activities that require the children to go slowly. It might not be fun, for example, to bake with a child who does not read the instructions and cannot pour with precision. But these are the very activities that the child needs to practice to improve the skill.

Active Skill Development

- to practice the ability to resist a temptation, urge, action, or impulse

Dance Freeze

Instructions

Grades K–3
Approximate Time: 30 minutes

1. Play music. Instruct students, "Everybody dance until the music stops!"
2. Music continues as you hold up a card with a stick figure on it. Make sure all the children see the card. If you don't have time to draw the figures on card stock before you start, draw them on the chalkboard or whiteboard in front of the students, or do the poses yourself.
3. Students look at the card but they do not strike the pose.
4. Stop the music ten seconds after you show the card; then students strike the pose.

Discussion Before and After

- Discuss what tools students used to wait to strike the pose.
- Reflect on how hard it was to do this activity. If it was hard, what similar activity at home do students also find hard?

Moment-to-Moment Support

Nonverbal Cues

If you know that a particular student will struggle with this activity, consider placing your hand on the child's shoulders and looking at him/her just before you show the card with the pose. Hold up a hand to signal *Wait*. This cue will remind the child to wait the five seconds before acting.

Grouping

Though this activity lends itself well to full-class activity, homogenous grouping of students of similar abilities is recommended. With students in smaller groups, the teacher can choose a speed of music and difficulty of each pose to better target each group's ability.

Self-Talk

Explain to students what it looks like to slow down and approach a task with focus and care. Verbally detail the concentration that you put into a task: "I have always loved sewing, but I find it hard to do. My hands normally move quickly so my movements aren't precise. I will slow down before I start. I can take a deep breath before I grab the needle, and this will help slow my movements down. I can look at the objects in my hands, before I start using them."

Detailed Positive Praise

We often tell a child to slow down and to stop and think, but we do this while the child is moving quickly. Instead of pointing out each time the child is moving too fast, praise the positive thinking. Instead of stopping the child every time he /she is moving without thinking, remark on when he/she does something slowly and carefully.

Redo

Try as often as possible not to tell a child to slow down or to get upset at his/her quick action. Rather, bring the child back to where he/she was just before he/she acted without thinking; encourage the child to try again to keep control of his/her body by walking slowly with deliberate thoughtfulness.

Homework

Send home a description of the activity. Include this suggestion:

> Help your child slow down at home. Be sure to support the desired behavior of your child when he/she moves quickly and without thought. Shadow him/her and help him/her stop on the spot and take one deep breath before moving.

Matching Movement

Looking Beyond the Behavior

In a student with weak skills in matching movement, you will observe
- failure to match the movement of the environment or others
- student is often out of sync with speed and movements of other children

Understanding the Skill of Matching Movement

In order to join seamlessly with a group, a child's body must be present in the space, matching the tone, movement, and pace of the other children. It is easy for adults to dislike this statement; we want to celebrate uniqueness and creativity. We might not like the idea of encouraging children to follow others and join in with them. But it is important to understand that children who can look to others and join in with their activity enjoy more successful play at recess and are, in turn, exposed to more social experiences from which to learn and grow. Children who are on the fringe of play, who walk alone at recess and walk away from the group, do not play as much at recess, miss out on social opportunities, and miss out on chances to learn and practice their play skills.

Active Skill Development

- to learn to observe others and follow their movements and patterns of behavior

Mood Dance

Instructions

Grades K–3
Approximate Time: 15–30 minutes

1. Load your mp3 player or pick CDs with different types of music.
2. Have students sit down or stand up around a room.
3. Play music and have students respond with their bodies with actions that match the music being played: e.g., actions could include yoga, slow stretches, aerobic activity, fast dancing, slow dancing, pretending to sleep.
4. Demonstrate a matching facial expression to go with the music.
5. Now have students move in a way that does not match the music: e.g., aerobic activity with romantic classical music.
6. Begin with very extreme music selections and slowly introduce music that is not extreme or changes melody during the song.

Discussion Before and After

- Discuss whether it is easy or hard to match one's movements and energy level to certain music.
- Discuss how odd it looks for the body's movements to contradict the tone of the music.
- Discuss the advantages and disadvantages of following the group and of not following the group. Help students understand when following a group is important, helpful, and advantageous. Talk about the problems that occur if someone always follows the group and does not think for him/herself or stand up to a group: e.g., bullying; not able to have his/her own ideas; not being creative and unique.
- Reflect on whether or not this activity was easy, whether they were uncertain as to how to match their bodies to the music.
- Reflect on whether they think they follow the actions of their friends. Do they often join in and copy their friends' actions? Or do they do whatever they want, whenever they want?

Moment-to-Moment Support

Verbal Thinking Cues

"This activity is not going too well right now and I think I know why. I see that the students in the class are all moving at different paces and not taking the movements and patterns of others into consideration. If we continue like this, we will not be in sync as a group. I think we all need to look around and consider how our classmates are moving for this activity."

Nonverbal Cues

Have students look at other students to match their movements. If a child walks out for recess slowly and without focus, point him/her to the children up ahead and encourage him/her to join the group.

Zone of Proximal Development

Look at the child and see which part of his/her body is moving slightly. Copy his/her movements first. Don't try to get the child to do want you are doing or what the other children are doing. Copy what the child is doing. Copy it for a while, so that the child feels safe and successful at what he/she is doing. Then add to what the child is doing, a slight extra movement that can be copied successfully. Don't tell the child to copy you. Simply show an added step to his/her movement. Look to him/her, then look at your added movement.

Self-Talk

Show students how you alter your behavior to match the needs of others: "I sure would like to walk right now, but I can tell that everyone in the class is running ahead to the baseball diamond. Sometimes I need to change my movements and follow the movements of others, so I will run too."

Homework

Send home a description of the activity. Include this suggestion:

> Connect your child's successes at home and at school. This is a partnership. If we want the children to be able to generalize skills, we need to be ale to share resources across the two environments. Share the music you use at home with me and find out what music is being used in class. If your child hears music repeated at home and at school, he/she will be more motivated, because it is something which he/she has more exposure to.

Alternating Movement

Looking Beyond the Behavior

In a student with weak skills in alternating movement, you will observe
- student struggles with transitions
- student has difficulty alternating and switching movements

Understanding the Skill of Alternating Movement

Some children are concentrating so hard on what they are doing they are unable to transition from one activity to another or from one room to another. This is often due to an excellent ability to focus, concentrate, and settle in on a task. However, when a child is told to put the task away and switch activities or leave the room, the child can become very upset. We can help children with transition challenges by consistently pausing, changing, and adapting their play in manageable amounts.

Active Skill Development

- to practice alternating and switching movements and activities in motion

Wave

Instructions

Grades 1–3
Approximate Time: 30 minutes

1. Have students form a circle.
2. The first strikes a pose. Make sure the student uses his/her whole body and shows emotion in his/her face. The student can look angry, sad, or scared.
3. In order around the circle, everyone copies and holds the pose.
4. Once everyone is holding the pose, the next person changes the pose.
5. Like a wave, each child changes pose when it is his/her turn, until everyone in the circle is holding the new pose.
6. Continue around the circle until everyone has had a chance to change the pose.

Discussion Before and After

- Discuss the advantages of watching friends and switching movements throughout the activity.
- Reflect on how hard it would be if you had to hold one pose for the whole activity, instead of switching and moving in different ways.

Moment-to-Moment Support

Grouping

Whole-class grouping works well for this activity. Make sure the first five children who lead the poses will be able to think of an original idea for a pose quickly, since they will not have as much time to think. Place children who need time to get used to the game at the end of the wave.

Detailed Positive Praise

"I am so proud of you, class. It can be challenging to look with the eyes and change from a movement we like to a different movement."

Peer Scaffolding

Place a creative and helpful peer before a child who struggles with this game. If the child with the weak skill does not change pose along with the others, cue the peer to turn his/her body to face the child, so that the child can see the pose more closely.

Proactive Explanation

Explain in detail the expectations of the activity and for after the activity, so that the student is completely aware of what he/she should do. Also explain to the student exactly how you will support him/her throughout the process.

Understanding the Skill Deficit

Concentrated, focused attention on an activity has many advantages in terms of productivity. However it can create serious challenges, especially in a classroom setting, which requires extreme flexibility of attention and has many transitions. Understand that what causes students (and you) challenges in one area might also be the source of a great strength.

Marsha

If Marsha is engaged in an activity that moving away from might upset her, her teacher proactively counts her down, stating how long the activity will be and when it will be over. Before beginning the activity, her teacher states in detail what with happen after the time is up: "After we are done drawing, it will be time to go to for lunch. When drawing is done, it is important that we stay calm and do not yell. If you yell and get upset, it will not change anything. We will not draw for longer and it will not change the schedule. " In time, the teacher has Marsha tell in detail how she will try to react when the timer goes off. During the activity, the teacher pauses the activity as often as he/she can, so that Marsha is able to start and stop her focus and engagement in the activity. As time goes on, peers can be used to create the short breaks for Marsha instead of it being solely the teacher's responsibility.

Self-Regulation

Looking Beyond the Behavior

In a student with weak self-regulation skills, you will observe
- student's body and energy level do not match the situation or environment
- student has a hard time identifying his/her body's energy level
- student does not connect his/her influence over physical behavior and ability to manage his/her own regulation
- student lacks sensory tools to calm down or be ready to learn

Understanding Self-Regulation Skills

Some children are not able to control their body's energy level or adjust their body's arousal level to meet the needs of the environment. In order for us to support these children, they must first have a cognitive understanding of the variety of energy levels and their appropriateness for different environments. They need to understand that their energy level should match that of the environment and that of their peers. Children need to be shown that they can change their body's energy level by changing the way they think about a situation and their control over it. Help children examine the relationship between feelings, thoughts, and actions and the impact they have on our bodies. We need to help them determine which self-regulation techniques work well for them.

Active Skill Development

- to learn to match the body's energy levels to the needs of the environment

Tools for Cool

Instructions

Grades K–6
Approximate Time: 30–45 minutes

1. Tell students you are going to work together figure out which activities work best to alert us when we feel tired or calm us when we feel hyper.
2. Use mats to define space or give each student a specific location in the room. Students are to stay in place and not run around or touch other students.
3. Have students run on the spot and act hyper, angry, energized.
4. At your signal (e.g., a whistle), everyone stops and copies you in a self-regulatory activity from the Self-Regulation Chart on page 59.
5. Do three Arousing activities in a row: e.g., kicks, dancing, skipping). Between each activity, have students walk one lap around the room.
6. Have students return to their places and color a picture or read a page from an age-appropriate book.
7. Ask students to think about how they feel; if it was easy for them to read or color, or if they were unable to concentrate. Give each a copy of the Self-Regulation Chart on page 59 and have them circle how they felt after each group activity.
8. Repeat the game using three Relaxing activities: e.g., yoga, breathing, stretch.
9. Repeat the game using three Heavy Work activities: e.g., pushups, lunges, weights.

It is important for students to perform an age-appropriate cognitive activity to recentre after the self-regulatory task. It helps focus their minds.

Throughout this book, shapes are used to show emotions and actions:

♡ Heart = what we feel

▭ Rectangle = what we do

💬 Speech balloon = what we say

💭 Thought bubble = what we think

Discussion Before and After

- Discuss how their bodies feel after each self-regulatory exercise.
- Reflect on which activities they found most calming.

Moment-to-Moment Support

Scaffolding

Have your own chart with you and make notes on particular students you are concerned about. Be aware that this activity will not give you real-life answers, because the break between activities is not long enough. This is simply a starting point, for you and for them, to understand that different activities can help increase or decrease our level of excitement.

Model

Model the activities you find helpful throughout the day. Stretch; bend down and touch your toes. Tell students that after lunch you feel tired and want to have a

Self-Regulation Chart

Type of Activity	Action	How Your Body Feels ♡		
Arousing	Lunges	Tired	Focused	Hyper
	Kicks	Tired	Focused	Hyper
	Cancan	Tired	Focused	Hyper
	Dancing	Tired	Focused	Hyper
	Skipping	Tired	Focused	Hyper
Relaxing	Mindful Breathing: • Breathe in deeply through your nose. Feel the breath come into your lungs. Pause and silently count to three. Now, let out your breath very slowly. Feel your breath leave your body. Repeat this 5 times. • Notice the muscles in your face. Relax them, beginning with your jaw. Next, relax your shoulders, feeling the tension melt away. Be aware of each relaxation. • Place both hands on your stomach to feel your breaths come in and out, in and out. Breathe in slowly and deeply, deep down in your belly. Then let out the breath slowly. Feel your hands go up and down with the air coming in and out of your body. Repeat this 10 times, watching your hands move up and down.	Tired	Focused	Hyper
	Progressive Muscle Relaxation: • Squeeze your toes. Release your toes. • Open your eyes wide, then close your eyes tightly. • Point your toes, then flex your toes. • Open your mouth, then shut your mouth. • Scrunch your cheeks, then relax your cheeks.	Tired	Focused	Hyper
	Yoga Poses: • Downward Dog • Warrior • Tree	Tired	Focused	Hyper
	Stretch: • Raise hands in the air • Roll shoulders • Leg stretch	Tired	Focused	Hyper
Heavy Work	Do 20 pushups	Tired	Focused	Hyper
	Turn to a partner and push on each other's hands	Tired	Focused	Hyper
	Sit back-to-back with a partner and try to push against each other's backs	Tired	Focused	Hyper
	Lift heavy books 20 times	Tired	Focused	Hyper

nap, but you have learned that a few quick stretches and moving your body up and down is just as helpful in preparing you to learn.

Detailed Positive Praise

Connect the tool to a student's level of alertness. "I think that Neil looks like he has washed his worries away. The relaxing activity has made you look calm and stress-free. Well done. What do you think about how you feel?"

Regulate the Environment

In math class, as the class gets squirmy, pull out the Self-Regulation Chart and have students pick one activity each to try. Have them perform the activity for three minutes and then return to work; ask them to think about whether or not the activity helped them for the last part of the class. Make notes and changes to the chart using real data from class. Use this information to help you work more effectively as a class.

Verbal Thinking Cue

"Self-regulation is the ability to match our bodies' energy level to our environment. If we are really hyper in class, we want to learn ways to calm ourselves. We all have different ways to calm ourselves and to help us relax. But it would be great if we could find one or two of these activities that we all found useful, so then we could do them between each subject, together as a group."

Movement Control

Looking Beyond the Behavior

In a student with weak movement control skills, you will observe
- inability to start and stop in motion on his/her own
- difficulty starting and stopping in motion in response to a request

Understanding Movement Control Skills

It is frustrating to watch as a child moves farther and farther away from us as we call to him/her to stop and join the group. It certainly feels like the child is choosing not to listen and is making an active decision to disobey. But if we stop to think about the energy in the classroom and the active movements of the children, we see that their focus on a different task and their active movement toward it (and away from us) makes more sense. Sometimes it is hard for a children to stop immediately and join in what we want them to attend to, mentally and physically. So the more often we encourage their movement while engaging them cognitively, and then get them to slow down, pause, or alter their movement, the more we will help them build an important skill.

Active Skill Development

- to practice starting and stopping in motion

Relay Race

Instructions

Grades 1–6
Approximate Time: 30 minutes

1. Set up a simple relay race with the material you have at your school. Give clear instructions and demonstrate. Start simply, since the challenge of this race is what you are adding to it.
2. Tell students that they have to count the number of times you clap, ring a bell, or blow a whistle while they run the relay. Once they start running, start clapping (or ringing or whistling). At first, make the sound very loudly, slowly, and in rhythm. You might start by counting with them.
3. They need to stop and perform a task, no matter where they are, each time the sound count reaches 10. The task should be simple and the ability appropriate. If you are doing this race with children aged six to nine, for example, they should simply stop and touch the ground.
4. Once they have performed the task, they return to the race and continue counting.

Add a focus or precision task (e.g., threading a needle, beading, ring toss, ball target, water-gun target) to the relay so that students have to run, then stop, slow down, and perform a slow and deliberate task.

Discussion Before and After

- Discuss how much effort it takes to think about moving your body while still thinking with your brain.
- Reflect on what would happen if you moved your body without thinking with your brain.

Moment-to-Moment Support

Peer Facilitation

Encourage peers in each group to do the counting, so that students are working without you.

Nonverbal Cues

Hold your hands up and count down on your fingers as you blow your whistle. At ten, flash your hands so that the student sees that you have reached 10.

Detailed Positive Praise

When you see a quick-moving child doing something slowly with thought or precision: "Lee, I can tell that you are motivated not to wreck the packaging of your playing cards. Because of that, you are removing the wrapper very slowly and with great care. If I am correct, you actually stopped and considered how to open before you moved. That is a great way to take care of your packaging for your playing cards. We can use those same slow skills of starting and stopping, to take care of other things in the classroom and at home."

Reward System

Consider making a Stop/Look/Think checklist for a student who does not tend to stop and slow down. Place the checklist somewhere accessible so that the child can give him/herself checkmarks each time he/she consciously slows down. Once all the checks are filled in, the sheet can be posted to celebrate the child's success.

Homework

Send home a description of the activity. Include this suggestion:

Alternate between counting for your child while he/she does the race and having your child count for you while you do the race.

3

Actively Developing Language Skills

Receptive Memory

Looking Beyond the Behavior

In a student with weak receptive memory skills, you will observe
- student is unable to receive and recognize auditory or visual information
- when given a direction or an instruction, student signals he/she will begin the task, but continues activity without adjusting behavior
- student does not move after instruction

Understanding Receptive Memory Skills

Receptive oral language is not simply the ability to hear the verbal sounds another person says; it is also the ability to input that information into memory (encode it), create a permanent record of the information (store it), and later retrieve it (recall it). In this case, the retrieval is nonverbal; i.e., the child shows what he/she knows, but does not need to access the word verbally and say it. For example, most children are able to jump immediately when an adult tells them to jump; they have successfully input, stored, and retrieved the word "jump." Another child might not jump when you say the word. If you jumped first, then looked at the child and said, "Jump," he/she would jump; however, the child is not using auditory language to perform the task, but instead is using visual skills to copy your movements. It is important to support this child by consistently pairing the auditory and visual; i.e., saying "Jump" while you jump. Just as importantly, this child needs to be exposed to the word without the visual in order to help build his/her receptive input abilities.

Active Skill Development

- to practice inputting information into memory (encode it), creating a permanent record of the information (store it), and later retrieving it (recall it)

Community

Instructions

Grades K–6
Approximate Time: 15 minutes

1. In a large, open space, have students run around freely, waiting for your key words.

2. Call out action words and have students perform the movement. Make the movements gradually more complex: e.g., "Skip," and then "Skip around the pylons."
3. Change to calling out characters. See list of Sample Characters and Movements below. Students need to mentally associate each character with a particular movement and perform that movement.
4. Introduce new characters and movements slowly. After each new character, repeat already-learned characters and words, so you are building vocabulary over time.
5. Encourage students to add their own characters and movements.

SAMPLE CHARACTERS AND MOVEMENTS

Rescue Hero: go to the closest wall
Circus Performer: leap over the lines on the floor
Old Man: walk slowly
Ballerina: jump on the spot while moving arms around
Cheerleader: do jumping jacks
Teacher: stand up straight with arms at sides
Taxi Driver: sit down
Magician: hop on one foot
Athlete: run around

Discussion Before and After

- Discuss what tricks different children use to help them remember which actions go with which words.
- Reflect on different situations that require people to use similar deductive and processing skills.

Moment-to-Moment Support

Scaffolding

Stand close to the students who struggle with this activity. If possible, whisper the movement word in a student's ear just before you call it out to the class. That allows him/her the extra few seconds needed to process the information.

Visual Support

Have a picture of each movement for the game on a sheet of paper. Show the picture to the students about one second after you say the word. It is important to say the word first, so that the weak skill is challenged before you provide support.

Learning Process

Don't reject rote learning as an excellent learning tool. Drill-and-repeat activities are essential in order to help children build associations.

Homework

Send home a description of the activity. Include this suggestion:

Support your child with this activity and any other pairing of movement and words. Do not show the action before or after you say the word. Have your child

A sentence like "Get ready for math" has multiple hidden commands in it: put your language books away; get your pencil, eraser, calculator, notebook, and text; move to a desk across the room where your group works.

do the action and then have him/her repeat the word while doing the action. You can join in the action once he/she has done it.

- You can increase the level of complexity of the words to suit the needs of your child. This might include using sentences.

- Practicing this will help build your child's ability to access these words in other environments. It is possible that your child will be much more successful with you at home in your backyard than at school in the gym. Practice the activity at home until the child is successful there. Then move the activity to another environment that is slightly louder and busier, and therefore more stressful. Keep trying in that environment until your child is successful there.

Processing

Looking Beyond the Behavior

In a student with weak processing skills, you will observe

- inability to complete tasks that involve inferences or to sort out information within the task
- student is not ready for a task, but does not take active steps to seek help or get materials
- student struggles to connect a command with the tasks that are associated with it

Understanding Processing Skills

Unfortunately, in life, we are not always given instructions with straightforward information. We are often given general statements with an enormous amount of implied information. Implicit in many directions is previously acquired and learned information: these are schema scripts. Each of us retains certain schemas scripts, frames of previously acquired information that help us organize our memories and comprehend information. If a child is told to go get a drink, the child has to know what system the class uses to have their drink in order to comply. Is there water in the class? If not, are children allowed to go into the halls? Do they use cups? Do they need a water bottle? What happens if the school uses water bottles but a child doesn't have one? Some children's schema scripts include all the implicit information; they are able to get the drink completely on their own. Some children know if they had a problem and self-advocate to get help, like letting the teacher know they need a water bottle. But other children will stare blankly at the teacher, thirsty, yet completely unsure of what to do to get the drink. The schema script for these children is missing the information necessary to complete a task that, to others, is very simple. Accommodations for these children ensure that we give them one-step, explicit instructions; however, in order to build this skill in these children, we need to support them with daily tasks that require accessing schema scripts.

Active Skill Development

- to learn to input information and then transform it by sorting it and associating it with previously acquired information, so that the information has been changed and has contextual value

Mixed-Up Simon Says

Grades K–6
Approximate Time: 15 minutes

Instructions

1. Explain that you are going to play a mixed-up version of Simon Says.
2. Start slowly, using two body parts. When you say, "Simon says, touch your head," students must touch their feet. When you say, "Simon says, touch your feet," students must touch their heads.
3. Allow students to practice this step multiple times.
4. Switch to two other body parts. When you say, "Simon says, touch your knees," students must touch their shoulders; when you say, "Simon says, touch your shoulders," they must touch their knees. Allow them time to practice this step multiple times.
5. When you think students will be successful, include more action steps. Encourage students to suggest which body parts to switch.

Discussion Before and After

- Discuss what mental tools they use to sort out the information in the instructions.
- Reflect on how hard it was to hear "touch your knee" and to stop and think about which body part that meant they were supposed to touch.

Moment-to-Moment Support

Grouping

Use small groups, with a student with weak processing skills as Leader. A child who struggles with the processing of this task might be great at calling out the Simon Says commands. Allow the child to act as Leader first, so he/she can observe and get a sense of the game before he/she needs to do it.

Structure

Have the students who struggle most at the task closest to the Leader. That way, they will be able to hear the command and not have to wait for the others and copy their movements.

Nonverbal Cues

Smile encouragingly and nod to the student to support his/her thinking.

Learning Process

Give the student time to answer any question. Don't talk for him/her, but wait patiently and let him/her know he/she has time to answer the question.

Peer Scaffolding

Whenever you have a list of instructions you know will be challenging for some of your students, pair children up so that they can work together to understand each step of a task. Tell the pair that you will list some steps that they will be doing later; together they write down the steps. If they can't remember the steps, they can turn to another pair for help; the other pair can tell them the steps orally, but not show them. Once they have the steps, each pair needs to read each step

We tend to rush children, to speak and act for them if their responses are not fast enough. Slow down, wait, and give the child time to process information and then speak or act. Given time, they can often do more than we think they can!

together and make sure they both understand the task—how to do it, where to do it, and why they need to do it.

Homework

Send home a description of the activity. Include this suggestion:

> You can keep adding more and more steps to this game. Consider matching different body parts each time, so that your child can't rely on memory from playing the game a previous day.

Understanding the Skill Deficit

Consider the routines with which the student struggles and create clear schedules, so that you will not be surprised each time the child needs support. We can help these children with simple visual schedules that detail their routines in pictures or words. Point to the schedule at the same time as you tell them to be ready for a task or situation, and it will help the child begin the steps.

Mindful Listening

Looking Beyond the Behavior

In a student with weak mindful listening skills, you will observe
- inability to demonstrate understanding using verbal communication
- student does not respond after a verbal instruction
- student can follow only a few steps in instructions
- student can hear but does not attend during the listening process
- student looks away and gets distracted while another person is speaking

Understanding Mindful Listening Skills

Listening is not hearing; it is not simply the skill of being able to hear sound. It is a process that involves our ears, our minds, and our emotions. There is a cognitive aspect to the listening process that involves hearing the information, being mindful in the moment, attending to the proper information, organizing and interpreting it, and responding to it verbally or nonverbally. When we look at all the skills it takes to listen, it makes sense that some children struggle to take in the verbal information and act according to instruction. We want to help children attend to multiple command statements and perform them. In some cases, children are listening and they do hear the information, but their brains do not process all the information required to complete the task. In class, we accommodate these children by letting them use their visual skills. Accommodating these children is an important part of teaching; however, do not miss opportunities to help children build these skills.

Active Skill Development

- to practice staying focused on information and staying in the moment with the speaker

Are You Listening?

Instructions

1. Have students sit in groups.
2. For each group, set a table with a few rows of small objects on one side. Have the same objects on the tables of each group. At the other end of the table put cups in a row.
3. Tell students that they must listen to all instructions before moving.
4. Give a list of silly instructions for a student to remember and repeat. Base the number of instructions on the students' ability to remember. The instructions can keep students at their tables, or can become movement instructions. (See samples below.)
5. Have the student repeat the instructions back to a friend before they start.
6. Once they are done following the instructions, ask students to repeat the instructions in reverse order to their friend.
7. Allow groups to create their own list of instructions and continue to do the same activity.

Make the steps more complicated by involving some processing and memory.

SAMPLE INSTRUCTIONS

Grade 1: "Take a blue block from the middle row. Get up and walk around the table, passing Jenny, not Bill. Put the block in the cup with red water. Sit back down."
Grade 3: "Take two blue GOGOs. Walk around the table counter-clockwise. Put one GOGO in a cup with a red flower sticker at the bottom, put the other GOGO in a cup with a sticker of your choice. Before you start, tell Jasmine which sticker cup you will put it in before you start."
Grade 5: "Touch the north, south, and east walls of the classroom. Go to the chalkboard on the west side of the class and write the answer to the question 4 x 5. Come back to your group and ask the tallest person in the group if you can sit in his/her seat."

Discussion Before and After

- Discuss how concentration and focus are required to attend to lists of tasks.
- Reflect on what students were doing in their heads to listen to the information and recall it.

Moment-to-Moment Support

Regulate the Environment

Modulate the pace of the game with your language's rhythm, intonation, speed, and pauses. If your classroom seems busy, there are multiple interruptions, and the energy seems to be increasing, slow your speech, stop talking, look, and wait. Try not to say, "Don't go yet, stop. I am talking. Slow down. Calm down. Relax." Simply give the instructions in a slower, calmer voice.

Peer Facilitation

Have students show each other the auditory learning tools that will help them succeed. For example, Marsha might do very well on a task like this and she could explain to another child the process she uses to remember the list.

Scaffolding

Be present in the groups to support a child who might need the verbal instruction paired with visual instruction.

Peer Scaffolding

Have students repeat the sentences back to each other twice before performing the actions.

Verbal Thinking Cues

Pair this activity with the concept of listening to complete instructions. Have a key word—for example, "Listening"—that you repeat before and after instructions. Explain the attention students need to use to concentrate and focus on game instructions, and tell them that the same energy to attend should be used when a teacher is explaining homework steps. Then begin to pair the cue with other lists of instructions, saying "Listening" before you begin a list of not-so-fun chores and encouraging students to use the same listening strategies.

Homework

Send home a description of the activity. Include this suggestion:

Support your child at home by helping your child use lists as his/her own learning tool. Play the same game but before your child can perform the tasks, have him/her write them down as a to-do list. If your child does not like to write or can't spell, you can scribe for your child. What is important here is teaching your child how to organize and sequence jobs. Write instructions as a simple, numbered list. Consider buying an agenda book so that you are writing the list the way your child needs to write homework for school.

SAMPLE LIST OF TASKS AT HOME

1. Do a somersault.
2. Jump on the trampoline 4 times.
3. Eat a candy.
4. Jump over the toy on the floor.
5. Walk backwards through the hallway.
6. Go outside singing "Who Let The Dogs Out?"
7. Swing on the monkey bars.
8. Watch your mom do a cartwheel!

Nonverbal Communication

Looking Beyond the Behavior

In a student with weak nonverbal communication skills, you will observe
- student does not look to others to send information
- student does not attempt to convey a message through gestures and facial expression

Understanding Nonverbal Communication Skills

In the absence of words, nonverbal communication must be used. Without words, messages can be communicated using signs, signals, gestures, nods, and looks. Socially, most of our communication is done nonverbally. We send our clearest messages and show our feelings through our bodies and our faces. We use pointing, showing, and movement to add detail to and improve the words we use. Some children do not use these strategies, because they are focused on a task or because they naturally are not tuned into the nonverbal nuances they can send and receive as a means of communication. Lacking the ability to look for and understand nonverbal messages has major academic and social implications. Children who do not understand the teacher's stern look telling them to stop what they are doing will not stop their actions; children who miss the friend who smiles, looks over at the slide, and points to it before running to it might think that their friend just walked away.

Active Skill Development

- to build the ability to understand a message sent through the body and face

Cat's Got My Tongue

Instructions

Grades K–6
Approximate Time: 30 minutes

1. Choose an activity for students to do in groups of two: e.g., build a block tower, scavenger hunt, draw a picture, complete an obstacle course, go through a maze, do a dance.
2. In each pair, one student is the Leader and the other is the Doer. The Leader is not allowed to talk. The Doer is the only one allowed to touch objects. The Leader can move around, gesture, show, but can't touch or speak to the Doer.
3. Together, students try to complete the task.

Discussion Before and After

- Discuss how important it is to look at and be patient with each other.
- Reflect on how difficult it was to communicate a message without words.

Moment-to-Moment Support

Nonverbal Cues
Go behind a child and point his/her shoulders toward the speaker. Gently tilt the student's head to look at the speaker.

Verbal Thinking Cues
"Sometimes we can't ask questions, so we need to use our eyes to get all of our information."

Chase the Skill

Where possible, do not do all the work for children who struggle to communicate. If you know a student's needs and anticipate what he/she wants, then you will be tempted to remove daily opportunities that he/she needs to communicate a message to you or to the other children in the class. Create the need for the student to get your attention and the attention of his/her peers. Be there to be sure that the other children are listening. Be there to move his/her body into the group so that he/she is looking at peers. Exaggerate the facial expressions he/she might need to make to communicate his/her message. The social interaction is and always should be about the child and the other children.

Homework

Send home these suggestions:

> Play Charades at home to create opportunities for nonverbal communication. Create categories for acting as a way to expose your child to many different subjects and ideas. Some children love animals and will always want to act out animals. This is great, but encourage a variety of actions: sports, superheroes, community helpers.

Intentional Verbal Communication

Looking Beyond the Behavior

In a student with weak skills in intentional verbal communication, you will observe
- student struggles to use words to explain him/herself
- student might have a large vocabulary but is unable to form sentences to explain his him/herself
- in group work, student struggles to explain thoughts in detail

Understanding Intentional Verbal Communication Skills

We have focused on the need to communicate with our friends using nonverbal means on page 70. All the same needs apply to the ability to use words to convey information or express ourselves. It can be difficult to recognize this deficit in some children. Children can have strong verbal skills and a great vocabulary, can speak for hours about a specific topic but, when asked to explain something they need or want or to explain what they are doing, they are unable to do so.

Children whose actual language is stronger than their ability to use it socially or emotionally could benefit from intervention with the autism team at your school and/or a speech pathologist who specializes in social communication instead of just articulation.

Active Skill Development

- to practice using language to send a message

Blindfolded Follow the Leader

Grades 1–3
Approximate Time: 30 minutes

Be sure to use simple actions and gestures. Some children struggle with basic action sequences and require time to process and replicate the action.

Instructions

1. Use the gym or a large safe playground. Order the students in line.
2. Blindfold all students but the Leader.
3. The Leader performs an action and gives directions in a loud voice so that all students can hear the action and replicate it.

Discussion Before and After

- Discuss the importance of giving detailed information to someone who can't see.
- Discuss the importance of volume and appropriate times to be very loud.
- Reflect on how difficult it was to move your body to verbal directions.
- Reflect on how hard it was for each student to describe actions in words.

Moment-to-Moment Support

Structure

Consider the space you have and think about how many groups you can have, if you can group by ability, and how you will order the line. If you begin with the fastest-moving students, they will rush ahead and you will lose your line. If you place the fastest children at the back, they might rush and push the line forward, putting pressure on a slower child and banging into each other. If you begin with one line as a class, the line will need to alternate between quick-moving and slower-moving children. If you encourage and supervise the line, your students will keep each other in balance in the line.

Regulate the Environment

It is important to understand the impact of stress on a child's ability to retrieve language and use it. If you are interacting with a student who is unable to communicate, explain, or describe at the level you believe he/she is capable of, it might not mean that the child is being lazy. If the room is noisy and busy, if the child is tired or excited about the next activity, or if the child is hungry, then he/she can't access the information he/she normally can.

Peer Facilitation

Peer-to-peer summaries teach children to speak peer-to-peer. For example, while working on a social studies chapter together, each student should be instructed to read a short section of the chapter. Then have students close the book and turn to face their partner. Partner A should summarize the material to the partner B. Partner B then repeats the important points that Partner A summarized and adds any details he/she wants to contribute. Partner A can then repeat the new details and information that Partner B added.

Expressive Communication

Looking Beyond the Behavior

In a student with weak expressive communication skills, you will observe
- student does not use language to provide information to another person
- student does not use language to send a message

Understanding Expressive Communication Skills

Some children are unable to use language to explain and convey a detailed message. These children are able to receptively input language, but are unable to expressively output the language they need to convey information to other people. For example, this child could hear you say the word "Jump" and would jump; he/she could see you jump, and would jump. But if you jumped and then asked this child what you did, he/she might not be able to access the word and say "Jump." The child was able to use his/her memory to recall the word to do it, but was unable to output it verbally to say it. These children struggle during play and group work. They are not able to explain their position, prove their point, or relay the information that they have.

Active Skill Development

- to practice using language to give detailed information to another

Tell Me What You Know

Instructions

Grades 1–6
Approximate Time: 30 minutes

1. Give students cards with sequenced instructions to draw a picture (see Sample Drawing Instructions on page 74).
2. Students work in partners: one is the Illustrator (gets information and draws the picture); the other is the Narrator (gives the instructions). Neither partner knows what the picture will look like.
3. Partners sit side-by-side, but the Narrator does not let the Illustrator see the instruction card. The Narrator gives one instruction at a time to the Illustrator, who draws the picture.
4. Give the Narrators simple pictures that they are not to show Illustrators. Repeat the activity with the Narrator giving step-by-step instructions from the picture.
5. Have students evaluate the work by looking at the picture together. Where was there miscommunication?
6. Have students write out the step-by-step instructions together.

Don't forget the point of this game. The final product does not matter. The goal is to demonstrate how hard it is to communicate to another person. If you see that students are having trouble and you get involved in their communication, they will not experience the miscommunication and they will miss the point.

Make a line across the page about one centimetre down from the top. Start on the left side of the page and go all the way across to the right of the page.	Put a circle the size of a dime in the very middle of the page. Draw a little square around the circle. Make the square as small as it can be without touching the circle. Draw a triangle pointing up, with a point at the middle of the bottom of the square. The lines of the triangle should go all the way to the bottom of the page. The triangle should not touch the corners, but come as close as it can to them. Complete the bottom line of the triangle.
In the top right corner of your page, draw a rectangle the size of a playing card. In the middle of that, draw a circle the size of a dime and color it purple.	Write the letter *B* in red in the bottom left-hand corner of your page. Just above it, draw a square the size of a dime. In the top left corner, draw 2 little butterflies.
In the top section of your page, draw a circle the size of an apple. Under the circle, attach a triangle of the same size that points up. Draw 2 lines coming out from the bottom of the triangle and one line coming out from each of the other sides of the triangle. Draw a small circle in the middle of the circle. Draw 2 more circles above the small circle and one U-shaped line under it.	Draw a line down the centre of your page from top to bottom. On the right-hand side of the line, in the middle of the page, make a circle the size of a tennis ball. Draw 4 lines coming out of the right side of the circle and 4 lines coming out of the left side of the circle.
Draw a small tree, the size of an action figure, in the middle of the page. To the right of the tree, draw another tree that is twice as big. Draw a river going down the page diagonally from left to right. In the bottom left-hand corner, draw a bear that is the size of a dollar coin.	Draw two lines down, from the top to the bottom of the page, dividing the page into three even sections. Draw a maple leaf about the size of an apple in the centre of the middle section.

Discussion Before and After

- Discuss the consequences of giving misinformation.
- Reflect on how hard it is to detail and describe simple information to another.

Moment-to-Moment Support

Praise the Learning Process

To reduce students' frustration, take the focus off the finished product. This activity is about how they share information, not what they accomplish. "Jenny, your explanation of the map is detailed and precise. When Glen was unsure, you slowed down and told him to move the green and brown car in between the fire hydrant and the tree, and it helped him know exactly where to put it. You gave a very detailed explanation. Good work." Praise should be about the process, not only about its results; try not to say things like "Well done, you got it right."

Do this activity as a class before you have students do it on their own. Have students give you instructions and you do the drawing. If you are a talented artist, do not draw above the ability level of your students. Show a level of work that you would expect from them. Demonstrating something they can achieve will increase their confidence in their ability to perform the task. While attempting to draw the picture, exaggerate confusion or misinformation. Don't correct the student giving you the instruction; make deliberate errors based on the information the student gives you. Play confused and model help-seeking language.

Peer Facilitation

Move from whole-class discussions to peer-to-peer discussion. For example, if you ask a question of the whole class, avoid having one student raise his/her hand and answer. Consistently facilitate peer-to-peer conversation by asking a question of the class and directing students to turn and face a peer. Have peers share their thoughts with each other.

Chase the Skill

Create opportunities to place the student in a situation where he/she must use language to get information. Use field trips and new teachers as chances for students who do not know the structure of the classroom to find information on their own.

Jenny

On a field trip, Jenny is looking around, unsure of where to put her backpack. The teacher does not rush in and ask the field-trip staff where the children should put their backpacks. Instead, the teacher walks up to Jenny and points to the staff. Verbally, the teacher can accomplish the same thing adult-to-adult. Instead, the teacher facilitated the student interaction.: "Jenny, I also do not know where we should put our backpacks, but I bet that person does. I would appreciate it if you asked her for me."

Perspective-Taking

Looking Beyond the Behavior

In a student with weak perspective-taking skills, you will observe
- student does not ask questions to find out about another person
- student does not understand that conversations are about two people talking back and forth

Understanding Perspective-Taking Skills

Some children lack the skill of taking perspective, the ability to see another person's point of view and to understand that the other individual has his/her own set of ideas, knowledge, and beliefs. Perspective-taking requires that we intuitively think about what other people are thinking and track what other people know, think, and feel during our conversations and interactions. Perspective-taking deficits result in communication difficulties, because the child does not understand that the other person holds valuable information, ideas, and thoughts in his/her head. The child does not comprehend that he/she must get an idea of what information another person already knows to understand what information the person needs to know. These children might walk up to someone and talk to them for long periods of time about a subject the other person already knows or does not care about. Conversely, they might not reveal important information or ask key questions because they assume the person already knows the information. This affects the ability of these children to chat with their friends and to grow their social friendships.

Active Skill Development

- to build the ability to see another person's point of view and to see that the other individual has his/her own set of ideas, knowledge, and beliefs

We Don't Know What We Can't See

Instructions

Grades 1–6
Approximate Time: 30 minutes

1. Students work with partners: one is the Sender of information; one is the Receiver.
2. Place a barrier between the Sender and Receiver. It can be a piece of cardboard, an easel, a big book. Or have students sit back-to-back.
3. Choose a task from the list below.

- Make a simple sequence or pattern: for example, stringing beads or putting colored blocks in a row.
- Color parts of a picture: color two identical pictures the same.
- Build a simple construction: for example, using Lego or blocks.
- Position items on a picture board: for example, "Park the green car in the small red garage."
- Detail the position of shapes or objects on a grid: for example, using a road map or Battleship gameboard.
- Find a route: for example, describing how to get from one point to another.
- Match images: for example, each partner has the same five pictures of cats; the Sender picks one and describes it so the Receiver guesses the correct picture.
- Pose: teacher makes a face or strikes a pose that the Receiver cannot see; the Receiver duplicates the pose or expression based on the Sender's description.

Before starting, help students understand what makes a good question and what does not. Write examples of questions that help us narrow down information and questions that would not help in the game.

4. The Sender must use words to give information to the Receiver to perform the task. Receivers are not allowed to look to get information, but should talk and ask questions.

Discussion Before and After

- Discuss how hard it is to determine what makes a good question and what does not.
- Reflect on a time when someone asked you questions to get information and you did not expand on or help them with your answers.

Moment-to-Moment Support

Detailed Positive Praise

"Sender, it looked like you saw that your partner was not getting what you were trying to say. You paused, thought inside your head, and then added more detail to your explanation. It was that extra bit of information you gave your partner that helped him/her figure out your message."

Peer Facilitation

If two students are miscommunicating during this game, or in any other activity, do not rush in to solve the problem or speak for the children. It is important to enter their space, look at each of them, smile, and nod. This shows them nonverbally that you are interested in them, that you are there for them, and that you can help. But your main efforts to help them should be to keep them calm and regulated. If the children are very upset, you might tell them to get a drink of water and then come back and sit down. This simple action might allow them to disengage mentally for a minute. Once they come back, your job is to help them communicate their confusion and misunderstanding to each other, not to see what one child is missing and explain it to the other. Help guide each child to see the other person's perspective: for example, instead of saying "What your Sender is trying to say is…" consider saying "I am not sure your Receiver understands what you are saying, so let's try again."

Homework

Send home a description of the activity. Include these suggestions:

> You will learn a lot about your child while playing this game one-on-one. If you are communicating to color in a drawing, does your child give detail? Can he/she explain where an object is? Does he/she understand how to use adjectives to give information? Is he/she creative and add interesting detail, or does he/she simplify each task? Will he/she follow your ideas and what you want him/her to draw or does he/she control the drawing and the way the game is played? How is his/her social interaction while playing? Where is he/she looking? What is he/she talking about—is he/she responding to your statements, comments, and questions? At each turn, catch your child's eyes and smile when you give a direction—get into his/her world and create social reciprocity.

Verbal Expansion

Looking Beyond the Behavior

In a student with weak skills in verbal expansion, you will observe
- student does not add comments to what another person says
- student contradicts what another person says
- student might engage in back and forth but, when the other person is speaking, does not appear to listen or maintain that person's topic of conversation

Understanding the Skill of Verbal Expansion

In some cases, instead of saying nothing, a child will say "No" or disagree before they think through what the other person has said. It can seem that they like to consistently disagree, argue, and correct. Promote supporting the thoughts of others by adding to their ideas by saying "Yes, and…"

As we teach children turn-taking in conversation and the back-and-forth of a discussion, we want to show them that we must be active listeners when it is the other person's turn to speak. It is not enough to let the other person speak; we must show them that we are really listening to him/her speak. This can be done by nonverbally showing interest; i.e., turning to, looking at, and nodding. But we must also verbally express interest in and agreement with their side of the conversation. One way to do this is to add to what they say while staying on the same topic. Without the skill of adding on, a child leaves the speaker feeling unheard. It helps to explicitly give children the sentences and lines to preface a comment or a statement when the other person has stopped talking.

Active Skill Development

- to practice adding a thought, comment, or statement to what another person has said

Yes, And…

Instructions

Grades K–3
Approximate Time: 30 minutes

1. Sit with students in a circle or at a table.
2. Write a conversation topic on paper, the chalkboard, or a whiteboard.
3. If you can, place items on the table to help build a conversation around a theme; for example, in the fall, place leaves, a mini pumpkin, mitts on the table.
4. Tell students what you will be talking about. Show students a conversation stick (any item you can hold in your hand) and explain that whoever is holding the stick will start a sentence with "Yes, and…," then add a thought about the subject.
5. Start by holding the conversation stick and leading with the first sentence. For example, "I like fall because of the feel of the wind on my face."
6. Pass the stick to the student beside you. He/she adds a *Yes, and…* comment to what you have said and passes on the stick.
7. For this activity to be successful, the students must listen to others and keep on topic. Lots of reminder items can help. Before you start passing the stick, you might talk about the topic with your students. You can list sentences that would be great to add and sentences that would not make any sense.

Discussion Before and After

- Discuss how enjoyable it is to have friends support and agree with what you say.
- Reflect on a time you were talking and the other person kept disagreeing with you and contradicting what you said.

Moment-to-Moment Support

Chase the Skill

Whenever it is appropriate, show the child you expect a response. Look to the child to show that you are waiting, hoping, and wanting them to add to what you just said. Wait for it—do not tell them what to say. Stop what you are doing and show that you want them to comment on what you said. Then give them time to process and add to your statement.

Peer Facilitation

Connect two children when you see that one is not listening to and adding to the ideas of others in a friendly and creative way. For example, prompt a peer to ask the student a question to help her comment: "Hannah, I think Jenny likes your idea. You could ask Jenny what she thinks about your explanation. It would be fascinating to hear what Jenny thinks about your ideas. I wonder if Jenny could add a *Yes, and...* comment."

Scaffolding

Use pre-made cards during class discussions. Some children need question cards to be able to participate in the classroom question period. Help students who do not participate in class by prompting them with cards they can use to add comments:
- "Yes, and I..."
- "That reminds me of..."
- "I like that too because..."
- "I also think that."

Homework

Send home a description of the activity. Include these suggestions:

> Use *Add a Comment* language at the dinner table. If you tell a story and your child does not respond to you or begins talking about something completely different, gently ask your child to "add a comment" to what you said. The more you do this, the easier it will become for your child. You can also write up a list of possible comments that can be made for most conversations. For a while, accept these simple and repetitive responses without pushing the child to say something more substantial. It is more important to teach your child to consistently look, nod, and make a simple comment than to worry about the quality of the comment. That will come in time.

Verbal Messaging

Looking Beyond the Behavior

In a student with weak verbal messaging skills, you will observe
- student uses a harsh tone or words when he/she disagrees with the group
- student is rude when others do not agree with him/her
- when children disagree in a group, student becomes very upset and snaps, yells, or says inappropriate things to group members

Understanding Verbal Messaging Skills

It is hard to work as a group. Disagreements in group work can be hard on friendships and can leave children feeling hurt and upset. It is often not the fact that the children had different opinions that creates real conflict; rather it is the way the discussion deteriorates. The glares and angry faces, the harsh tone of voice, and the language used once the disagreement starts is the real issue, and can even get children into trouble. Children need to be explicitly shown that they are allowed to disagree with their friends if they are able to do it in kind and considerate ways. They need to be given examples of sentences to use during conflict. It helps to practice these sentences on an issue that children do not care about.

Marsha

This activity might not work if an issue that Marsha consistently gets very upset about is used. Emotionally, she will not be able to calm herself and practice the activity itself. The teacher needs to pick a discussion topic that Marsha does not care about to help her gain the words and tools to politely disagree with others when she is not invested in the topic.

Active Skill Development

- to build the ability to monitor the nonverbal and verbal tone and signals in a conversation

Group

Instructions

Grades 3–6
Approximate Time: 30 minutes

1. Sit with students in a circle or at a table. Discuss the conflicts that arise during group work and their challenges with working in groups. Help students identify that communication is as important for working well as a group as agreeing and disagreeing with friends. Help them understand the verbal and nonverbal message we want to send our friends in the group: *I am not sure I agree with you, but you have the right to your opinion. I am ready to listen to your ideas and then I want to be able to share mine.*
2. If you are working with young children, you could do this activity nonverbally. Using the chart below, list and show the facial expressions and actions that would help the situation and those that would not.

Does Not Help Work in a Group	Helps Work in a Group
Glare at group members by staring in their eyes	Look back and forth to each member with soft eyes
Open your eyes big and wide in shock	Keep eyes slightly open and soft
Scowl	Smile
Move your hands a lot	Keep your hands at your side
Try to grab materials and take things	Keep your hands to yourself

Move your body a lot	Keep your body seated and still
Leave the group	Stay at your seat
Use a harsh tone	Use a soft tone of voice

3. When working with older children, you can use more complex verbal messages, as in the chart below.

Upsets Group Members	Does Not Upset Group Members
"You are totally wrong."	"We could try it again, but I have tried that before and I don't think it works."
"I hate it when you say that."	"Let's try to focus on the project."
"I don't like working with you."	"This project is hard, isn't it?"
"I am right. I know I am."	"I wonder if we could try it this way."

Use the template on pages 82–84 to copy and cut out sentence starters. Glue a craft stick to the back so students can hold them up.

4. Once you have finished writing examples on the board, provide students with sentence-starter cards (see pages 82–84). Or they can make their own. These give students something to have in their hands to remind them what they want to say when they do not agree with an idea. You can place these cards on a child's desk or around the classroom, and have them available for regular group discussions.
5. Write a conversation topic on the chalkboard or whiteboard.
6. Have students work in groups to discuss the topic using the sentence-starter cards. Students should not be raising their hands to talk, but instead holding up a sentence starter to add to the group discussion. If two students reach for their sentence starters at the same time, help them decide who will talk first.
7. Once students have practiced contributing to the group discussion using the sentence starters, have them try to expand the conversation without the preselected sentences.

Discussion Before and After

- Discuss how, when someone disagrees with you, it is not as upsetting when they are relaxed, they smile, and they say it in a calm tone of voice.
- Reflect on a time you were able to disagree with someone while managing to control the tone of your voice and the words you chose to use.

Moment-to-Moment Support

Model

Soften your voice and slow down the pace when you are discussing anything with your students that is challenging or involves a disagreement.

Self-Talk

Show students that you catch yourself using a harsh tone of voice and that you are capable of a redo: "Oh, I think that what I said came out sounding a little angry or maybe slightly rude. I will repeat my statement in a softer, kinder voice, and then

Sentence Starters

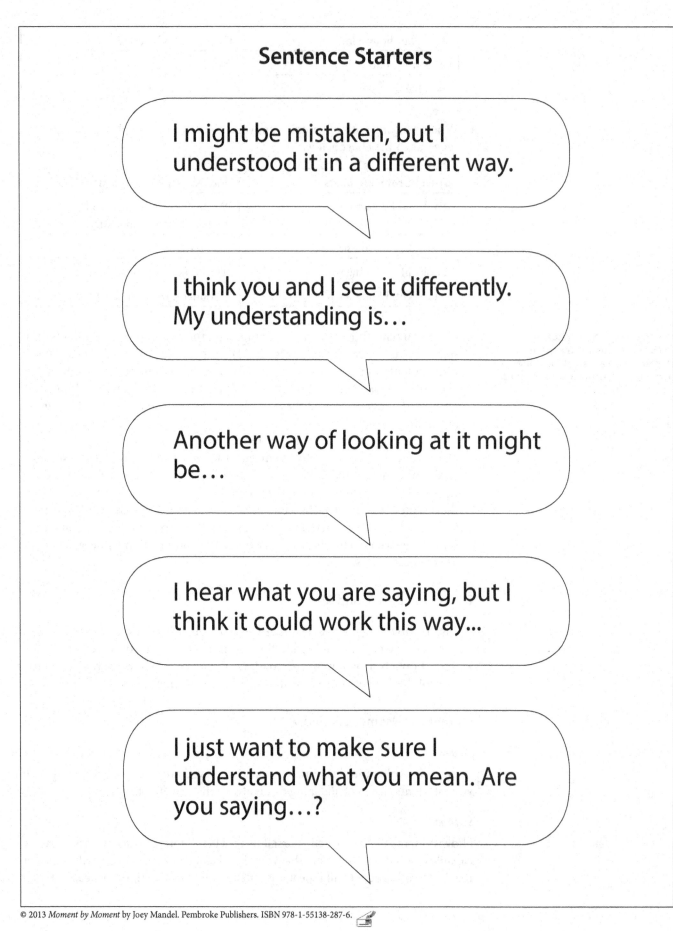

I might be mistaken, but I understood it in a different way.

I think you and I see it differently. My understanding is…

Another way of looking at it might be…

I hear what you are saying, but I think it could work this way...

I just want to make sure I understand what you mean. Are you saying…?

Sentence Starters (continued)

I am not sure that I got my point of view across. Could I try to explain it one more time?

I am not sure I follow you. Could you explain it in a different way?

Are you saying…?

I like your first idea. I wonder if we can brainstorm a little more about the second part.

I think that we have different ideas. Let me hear yours one more time. Then I will explain mine to you.

Sentence Starters (continued)

Yes, that makes sense, but I am not sure if it solves the problem.

I am not sure, but let's give it a try.

Can you explain what you think one more time?

I would like a chance to tell you what I am thinking.

I think I see this issue from another point of view.

try to continue the discussion staying calm. We can disagree about a topic, but I should try my best not to disagree in a rude way."

Verbal Cue

Repeat the sentence to the student in a kind tone of voice.

Peer Facilitation

If students are having a disagreement, support them and help them remain calm during the discussion. Let them know that they can discuss any issue with each other, but that everyone's first priority is to stay calm. Take your time: have students sit down in order to have the discussion; stop the discussion every few minutes for them to take a deep breath; repeat their sentences in soft tones and smile encouragingly.

Storytelling

Looking Beyond the Behavior

In a student with weak storytelling skills, you will observe
- student struggles to tell a story verbally
- stories do not include a beginning, a middle, and an end
- student has difficulty writing a story, especially when given a non-preferred story starter

Understanding Storytelling Skills

Using visual narratives to help children explain a real-life conflict they have experienced at recess or in the classroom, you can incorporate the emotional learning you are covering in class. Once children get used to using the visual narrative to describe their social events, they can use the same tool in their creative writing.

We need to help children take thoughts and ideas and put them into a story. Some children struggle to write a creative story. When they are asked to write, the task itself overwhelms them and they are unable to begin. Using visual narratives and working step-by-step, we can help children begin the writing process and learn to narrate a story verbally and through writing.

Active Skill Development

- to practice putting detailed story events into narrative order

Visual Narrative

Instructions

Grades 1–4
Approximate Time: 30 minutes

See page 88 for a template for the storyboard. Copy it onto 11″ × 17″ paper, or the largest sheets available.

1. Determine with the student what challenging event he/she would like to write about.
2. Draw a three-frame stick-figure storyboard to match what is described to you, showing a beginning, a middle, and an end. This can be a fictional story or a real-life problem.

SAMPLE STORYBOARD

| Beginning | Middle | End |

3. Write the events of the story based on the pictures.

SAMPLE STORYBOARD AND EVENTS

Beginning	Middle	End
Jenny has a bad hair cut.	Billy sees her and says hi.	Jenny is happy that Billy did not make fun of her.

Title: *Friends make their friends feel good.*

4. Add a title once the drawing is complete.

5. Add symbols to the drawings to help expand the story. Go back to the written story and add words to explain the detail of the story.

Use speech balloons, thought bubbles, and hearts to prompt the student to include what is said, what is thought, and what is felt.

SAMPLE EXPANDED STORY

Beginning	Middle	End
Jenny has a bad hair cut. She feels so embarrassed. She is worried that her friend Billy will make fun of her.	Billy sees that Jenny looks sad. He thinks she might be sad about her funny hair cut. Billy decides to says hi instead of making fun of her.	Jenny is happy that Billy did not make fun of her. She asks him to come over and play in her backyard.

Title: *Friends make their friends feel good.*

6. Put the parts of the narrative together into a written story.

SAMPLE STORY

> *Friends make their friends feel good.*
>
> *Jenny has a bad hair cut. She feels so embarrassed. She is worried that her friend Billy will make fun of her. Billy sees that Jenny looks sad. He thinks she might be sad about her funny hair cut. Billy decides to says hi instead of making fun of her. Jenny is happy that Billy did not make fun of her. She asks him to come over and play in her backyard.*

7. Act out the story as a play.
8. Get a new piece of paper and redraw the story using the detail you added in the play.
9. Write the story again, adding details from the new pictures.

Discussion Before and After

- Discuss how the pictures helped the student tell the story.
- Reflect on what it was about the drawings that made it easier for the student to organize his/her thoughts.

Moment-to-Moment Support

Zone of Proximal Development

It is important to truly understand that a student with this skill deficit cannot retell, write, or explain his/her story. The child is stuck, overwhelmed, and unable to put thought to paper, just as another child would not be able to do complex fractions. Our support for the student must take the form of a clear, manageable step in the writing process that he/she is able to do. Help the child with the drawing in order to get the next idea for the text. Help the child act out the skit in order to get the next drawing idea.

Praise the Learning Process

A mistake we often make, when teaching students to write, is to finish one story and start a new one too quickly; we value quantity over quality of writing. The advantage of using storyboards is that the student can rework the same story over and over again, focusing on the process: draw, write, act. Each time the student acts out the story, he/she will add detail. A student can work through the process three or four times with the same story. The final finished project will have excellent detail and expanded ideas.

Scaffolding

Support the student by showing the writing process at his/her level. Good visuals use pictures that match the language level of the child. If you show children images first, be sure to use simple pictures that are slightly more advanced than a picture the child could produce on his/her own. You might be an accomplished artist, but you cannot help a child learn to draw by showing something that the child could never reproduce on his/her own. Remind yourself that simple drawings are easier to comprehend.

Storyboard Template

Title:

4

Actively Developing Social Skills

Joint Attention

Looking Beyond the Behavior

In a student with weak joint attention skills, you will observe
- student is more object-focused than peer-focused
- student is more motivated to play with a toy than with a peer
- when playing with another child, student looks at the toy instead of the other child

Understanding Joint Attention Skills

The process of paying attention to the same thing as a social partner at the same time is called joint attention. In its simplest form, a child looks at another, then points to and looks at a toy, then looks back at the partner to make sure the partner sees what he/she sees and wants to engage in playing with the toy together. This process of joint attention leads to joint play. Their natural instinct helps children make sure they are playing the same way as other children, that they pass a toy to their play partner, and that they wait to see how the other child moves in play. It helps them follow the play of the other child. Without this natural instinct, children will struggle each time they play. Without joint attention, children become focused on their own play and stop looking to see how their play partner is playing and, more importantly, feeling. As school moves from play on the carpet to group work, a lack of joint attention continues to create social challenges: children who lack joint attention might become focused on the content of a project, but do not look around the group to check in with peers, hear their ideas, or see their frustration when their input is ignored. Joint attention skills are required in order to collaborate with a group.

Active Skill Development

- to build the ability to pay attention to the same thing at the same time as a social partner

Limbo Balloon Volleyball

Instructions

1. Divide activity area into two sides by putting a rope or string on the ground.
2. Students pair up; one partner sits on each side of the rope line.
3. Have students pass a large beach ball or balloon back and forth across the line. The goal is for each pair to pass the ball to each other and keep it off the ground. The focus of this game is tracking the ball and making eye contact with the partner each student is passing to on the other side.
4. As students play successfully, you can slowly raise the level of the string.

Discussion Before and After

- Discuss how players need to make eye contact with the partner across the rope to let them know that they are going to pass the ball to them.
- Reflect on how hard it was to look to a player and then look at the ball and make contact with it.

Moment-to-Moment Support

Grouping

Pair a student who will be strong at this activity with one who will struggle. This activity can also be done in multi-age groups. Since a child who struggles with this activity will lose confidence and self-esteem if paired with a peer who is much better at it, build this child's confidence by allowing him/her to be the more skilled partner by playing with a younger child.

Verbal Thinking Cues

"Even before you pass the ball, you need a signal from your friend to confirm that you will pass them the ball and to make sure they are ready to receive it. You can nod to your friend to let them know to pass the ball."

Praise the Learning Process

Play without counting or keeping track of points. Do not make this a competition between pairs. Focus on the language that each pair of children uses toward each other. They should enjoy the play together and encourage each other.

Nonverbal Cues

Point and show a child where to look, where to throw the ball, and how to nod to his/her partner to signal his/her intention to throw the ball.

Peer Facilitation

Do not get between children while they are interacting. Do not come in as the adult and speak to one child, then speak to the other. Stand behind one child and keep their attention on each other, not on you.

Regulate the Environment

Consider which objects facilitate sharing and social engagement and which objects hinder it. Some children have strong preferences and attachments to certain objects. A child can enjoy playing with trains so much that he/she begins to focus on the trains more than the play partner and the interaction. Upon closer examination, you might also notice that the child becomes so fixated on the trains that he/she becomes upset while playing with trains: the toy is preventing positive social interactions instead of enhancing them. If this is observed, you might remove the preferred toys from a part of the room: without them, the child might be calmer and more willing to share toys that he/she is less interested in. Do not remove the preferred items entirely, as they can be helpful as motivators for non-preferred activities: for example, in gym activities you can use the concept of trains as different forms of movement if the child does not like gym class. Do consider decreasing or restricting preferred objects as play objects when you want children to share space and interact together.

Social Reciprocity

Looking Beyond the Behavior

In a student with weak social reciprocity skills, you will observe
- student moves, plays, talks in his/her own world without back-and-forth with others
- student plays on his/her own, without giving, showing, handing to, or looking at peers

Understanding Social Reciprocity

Social reciprocity is the back-and-forth and give-and-take of social interaction. It includes all the social behaviors seen when two individuals are relating to one another: eye contact is shared; smiles are returned; gestures are interchanged; conversation builds and flows; and turns are taken. Social reciprocity takes two, with each person responding to the other immediately and in a way that takes into account what the other person just did. Some children lack the ability to maintain this natural back-and-forth, both nonverbally and verbally. They do not look to the other person to show they are listening; they do not nod in agreement or to acknowledge the speaker; in conversation, they might not participate, comment on, or respond to the statements of others; when they do speak, they might engage in a monologue, without making sure the other person is listening and having a turn to comment.

Active Skill Development

- to practice engaging in the back-and-forth and give-and-take of social interaction

Get Them to the Other Side

Instructions

Grades K–3
Approximate Time: 15 minutes

1. Divide an activity area into two sides with half the students on each side.
2. Scatter small balls or bean bags over the whole area.

3. Students try to clear their side of the balls by throwing the balls to the other side. As one side clears their balls, they are receiving balls from the other side!
4. Encourage students not to throw the balls at the other children, to keep the balls low, and to stay back, so as not to get hit with the balls.

Discussion Before and After

- Discuss how, every time they cleared balls, they got more back from the other side.
- Reflect on the fact that they had to use their eyes to look around their area while also looking at the other side of the room to see how many balls were on the other side.

Moment-to-Moment Support

Grouping

Before starting the game, create two equal teams with mixed-ability grouping. But consider the interaction between the groups, and place a quiet or withdrawn student on one side with a student who seeks social reciprocity and actively engages with peers on the other. Cue the social student to enagage with the quiet one.

Verbal Thinking Cues

"Every time you send a ball to a the other side, it gets sent back to you. Back-and-forth, back-and-forth, just like friendships!"

Peer Facilitation

Some students might stand still and not move in this game. Instead of helping the student yourself, have peers on the team hand him/her a ball.

Self-Talk

"Hmm, this ball just got thrown over to my side. I had better walk over and get it. I want to send each ball back over to the other side. I want to return each ball that someone sends me. If not, I will have all the balls on my side."

Homework

Send home a description of the activity. Include these suggestions:

Before starting this game, begin with a simple version of throwing. Have your child sit on the opposite side of the room from you. Your child should begin with all the bean bags (or balls, or stuffed animals) and you should have a large bowl, box, or bucket to use as a catching mitt. Once all the balls are in the catching mitt, switch so that you are throwing to your child. This is a wonderful way to help your child learn to follow a ball and catch it. While playing this game with your child, smile and nod. Laugh with your child and share the enjoyment of the game.

Imitation

Looking Beyond the Behavior

In a student with weak imitation skills, you will observe
- student does not look to another child and copy his/her movements
- student does not move in relation to others
- student has a hard time sharing space with others because he/she does not look to, copy, and react to the movements of another

Understanding Imitation Skills

The bodies of friends need to move together in relation to each other. Children need to be able to adjust their bodies to the subtle movements of others to be able to share space and create the back-and-forth of social interaction. If one child moves toward an object, other children will often copy that movement and follow the child into play. This action–reaction movement is a huge part of non-verbal play. In order to engage with and play well with peers, a child has to be present in the space with the other children, looking where they are looking, doing what they are doing, and eventually saying the same things the others are saying. Without this skill, the child walks off in play, moves out of play, and does not react in sync with the other children during play.

Active Skill Development

- to develop the ability and motivation to look to another person and copy his/her gestures, movements, and actions

Mirror Me

Instructions

Grades K–3
Approximate Time: 15 minutes

Control the speed at which students move their bodies with music. Instead of saying "Slow down" or "You are moving too fast," play soft, slow, rhythmic music and help students match their movements to the music to pace themselves.

1. Pair up students; have partners stand arm's length apart, facing each other.
2. Tell children that one partner will lead in actions and the other will copy. They can move their bodies, but they cannot move from their spots.
3. Suggest arm and shoulder movements. Focus on facial expressions: e.g., showing emotions, moving the mouth, rolling the eyes, scrunching the eyes, winking, turning the head.
4. Encourage the leader to move into his/her partner's space, so the partner needs to copy and move in even closer.
5. Move on to having students speak in pairs. Partners stand still but verbally repeat each sentence the other one says.

Discussion Before and After

- Discuss how they felt when their partner came into their space. Was it uncomfortable?
- Reflect on how close each student stands to people when talking. Does he/she get in the person's face or stand far away?

Moment-to-Moment Support

Nonverbal Cues

Stand right behind a child who struggles with this skill and manipulate his/her body so that he/she is looking toward the partner. Move his/her shoulders to toward the partner. Move his/her face so that he/she looks to the peer. Do not talk or use words; simply reposition the child's body. Use this same technique during table work, when the child is not working and talking with his/her group.

Chase the Skill

Exaggerate physical movement with students. Copy, move to, and react to their movements. Let them know what you are doing by explaining in detail the reason and purpose for your actions. For example, "You moved your body toward to the toy, so I will move with you toward the toy. Now you pulled back, so I am pulling back as well. I am following your movements."

Redo

If a child comes into the play of others and takes over, consider guiding the child back. Suggest that together you observe the movements of the group before deciding what to do.

Peer Facilitation

During peer work, partners can be disconnected. Students sometimes sit far away from each other and do not look at or face each other. Take your time helping children set up before they speak or work with a peer. Instead of general verbal directive statements and questions—for example, "Get started" or "What have you guys done so far?"—teach them how to begin working together. For example, "I see that you two have not begun talking to each other, brainstorming, or sharing ideas. It looks to me like you are not ready to begin working as partners. Working with a peer means moving your whole body toward your friend. Your hips, shoulders, and face should be facing each other. Your eyes should be looking at your classmate's eyes. And while your friend talks, you want to nod in agreement and encouragement."

Social Referencing

Looking Beyond the Behavior

In a student with weak social referencing skills, you will observe
- inability to speak to a person while looking him/her in the eye
- student looks away while speaking to a person
- student seems physically disengaged from social interaction or conversation

Understanding Social Referencing Skills

Social referencing is looking at another person, especially while speaking to him/her. A child might walk into a room, look right at you, and smile, but this same child might not be able to hold that gaze for a prolonged period of time, especially during a social conversation. Children who struggle to look their friends in the eye and make eye contact, especially during conversation, are judged as rude or not interested when, in fact, they are challenged in this skill. It is a sensory issue and needs to be respected as something that a child truly struggles with. However, this skill can be slowly and carefully encouraged and built through systematic desensitization and practice: not by telling the child to look at you while in class, but by helping the child practice the skill, especially at home or in a calm environment. Never tell a child to look you in the eye, but consistently try to encourage it; reinforce the child with a huge smile each time he/she looks at you.

Active Skill Development

- to practice looking to another person in order to engage with them socially

Mirror Me in the Eyes

Instructions

Grades K–3
Approximate Time: 15 minutes

1. Help students find partners with whom they will work well.
2. Have students stand an arm's length apart and facing each other.
3. Tell them that one partner will lead and the other will copy. They need to keep their bodies completely still. The only movement they are copying is the movement of the eyes.

This game is the same as Mirror Me on page 93, but focusing on the eyes. The whole body should stay still. It is only the eyes that students are mirroring.

4. Suggest eye movements; for example, they can wink twice with the left eye, then three times with the right eye; close both eyes; roll eyes; open eyes wide in surprise, then glare with them in anger.
5. Move on to having children add speaking while playing: singing songs, then talking about their favorite subject, then holding a back-and-forth conversation while continuing the game.

Discussion Before and After

- Discuss the importance of looking someone in the eye when speaking.
- Reflect on how students feel when they talk with someone. Where does each student look?

Moment-to-Moment Support

Grouping

To begin, this activity is best done with a student teacher paired with the child with the skill deficit.

Know the children in your class and consider their skills levels when grouping them. Pair a student who needs help with this skill with one whose development is further along and, even more importantly, whose temperament will not create too much sensory input that will frustrate the child with the skill deficit.

Jenny

This game would likely be hard for Jenny. She might be able only to mono-process: she would not be able to talk and look at the same time. Therefore, she would need to be paired with a child who was calm in nature, was soft spoken, and would engage in this activity slowly.

Since this activity works to expose a child to a sensory challenge that could overwhelm, be sure to decrease all other sensory input. Do not play this game in a busy hallway just before gym class as a fun activity to pass time. It might be fun for the children in the class who find it easy, but this activity is mentally draining for the child who struggles with this skill. So be sure to mitigate other sensory inputs that could make this activity too hard for the child it is designed to help.

Model

If students seem to be repeating the same movements over and over again, pause the game for a moment; if you are playing music, pause the music as a signal for the children to stop moving. Have each pair model one unique movement. This will provide multiple examples of new movements that each pair can work from.

Homework

Send home a description of the activity. Include these suggestions:

> You can slow it down and practice the activity nightly, but only for a few minutes. Consider doing the activity using body movements for five minutes and then focus on the face for one minute. If this is still difficult for your child, take a step back to create more distance between you, decreasing the sensory input.

Chase the Skill

Always chase this skill nonverbally and with caution. Do not come too close, stare right at the child, force your eye contact, or make verbal commands like "Look at me while I am talking to you." Simply find opportunities to come into a child's space slowly, to pause, to look at them, and to smile.

Social Observation

Looking Beyond the Behavior

In a student with weak social observation skills, you will observe
- student does not look to get information about what other children are doing
- student does not observe the reactions or gestures of other children

Understanding Social Observation Skills

In this game, children focus on being social observers. Children who observe what other children are doing, feeling, and thinking before coming into a group will be able to join the actions of the group more successfully than children who are not aware of what the group is engaged in. Sometimes a child might feel that nobody likes him/her or wants to play with him/her; however, the fact is that the children were playing, for example, hockey when the one child asked them to play tag. None of the children wanted to switch to tag, but did welcome the child to play hockey with them. This child with weak social observation skills does not first observe the actions of the group and consider that coming into their play requires joining what the group is doing, not trying to change the group's activity.

Active Skill Development

- to develop the ability to look to another person and the social environment in order to take in information

Observer

Instructions

1. Students sit at their desks or in a circle.
2. Have one student leave the room or close his/her eyes. This student will be the Guesser, who tries to figure out what changed in the group.
3. While the Guesser cannot see, or is out of the room, one student changes one thing: e.g., puts on a silly hat, puts on the teacher's coat, turns his/her shirt inside out, takes off a shoe.
4. Bring the Guesser back in the room or have him/her open his/her eyes. He/she looks around and tries to figure out who and what has changed.
5. Next, partner children and have them form two lines with partners in separate lines facing each other. On your signal, students turn around so that they are facing away from their partners. Each student changes three things about him/herself. On your signal, students turn back to face their partners. Each student must guess what is different about his/her partner.

Discussion Before and After

- Discuss the importance of observing friends.
- Reflect on how observant each child thinks he/she was in the game.

Moment-to-Moment Support

Grouping

For this activity, pairs should match on two abilities: the ability to come up with creative ideas for what to change, and the ability to spot change in the partner. A child who is strong in one of these skills will likely be strong in the other, but this is not guaranteed. The pairing will not be successful if one child is very creative and subtle with what he/she switches while the other child is unable to observe slight variations in his/her partner.

Praise the Learning Process

"I like the way some of you are taking your time with this activity. I think I saw someone notice something different right away, but waited before calling it out, looking up and down first to make sure that he/she was making the right guess. I think we are learning that it is not always about getting the right answer the fastest, but about the way we get our information."

Self-Talk

"This activity sure is hard for me. I am having a hard time trying to see what is different about my partner. I think it might be because I am only looking at his/her face. I keep thinking that, if I look harder at his/her face, I will see something different. But I think I need to look over his/her whole body—the shoulders, arms, even the shoes. I can't observe all of someone by staring at the same place."

Scaffolding

Some students need support through recess processes. Sit down with the student and write out a Play Plan for recess success (see sample below). After recess, have the student write a Play Report listing what went well and why. Remind the student of the Play Plan just before recess starts. Do not assume that the student will be able to apply what you reviewed the day before.

SAMPLE PLAY PLAN

> **STOP:** Before rushing into a group, I need to wait.
> **LOOK:** I need to observe the group first and see what they are doing.
> **LISTEN:** I need to listen to what they are saying.
> **PLAN:** I need to think of one thing I can say or do that matches what they are doing and saying.

Emotional Sharing

Looking Beyond the Behavior

In a student with weak emotional sharing skills, you will observe
- student does not seem to notice the emotions or needs of others; does not react when another child is upset or in trouble.
- student hyper-reacts to the moods of others

Understanding Emotional Sharing Skills

For social success, children need to be able to recognize the moods of others and react appropriately. In learning to imitate an emotion they see in another, children are not only observing the emotions of other people, but they are also learning to take on the emotions of others. If other children are laughing and having fun, a child must be able to join that group with excitement and joy. If someone is hurt and crying, a child who slows down and shows sadness is seen as kind and empathetic because his/her behavior changed in reaction to the emotions of another person.

Active Skill Development

- to learn to match one's mood to the mood of others and the demands of the situation

Your Feelings, My Feelings

Grades 1–6
Approximate Time: 15 minutes

Instructions

1. Students sit at their desks or in a circle.
2. Choose a Guesser to leave the room.

For some reason, we do not prioritize helping a child during recess as much as through other aspects of the curriculum. Recess affects the emotional well-being of a child and therefore should be supported: we should help them before, during, and after recess, just as we would help a child before, during, and after writing.

3. Choose a Leader to act out emotions for the other students to copy: e.g., sadness, happiness, surprise, disgust, interest, fear, anger, depression.
4. Bring the Guesser back into the room. He/she must try to figure out who the Leader is. Then the Guesser joins the other students in copying the Leader's emotions.

Discussion Before and After

- Discuss how much thinking is required from the Leader to keep inventing new emotions.
- Discuss how students need to be observant to follow the Leader, and tactful so that the Guesser does not see them looking at the Leader.
- Discuss how hard the Guesser has to work, using his/her eyes and being an emotional detective to find the Leader.
- Reflect on how each student reacts when someone is crying or angry. Are they sad or are they laughing?

Moment-to-Moment Support

Praise the Learning Process

Describe in detail the effort of each student to look to another and copy another person's emotions.

Neil

This activity would be excellent to help Neil consider the feelings of others and feel what other children feel. In this activity, Neil should be praised for any attempt he makes to look around the room. Descriptive praise should be used to provide Neil with information about his actions. For example, "Great work, Neil. You are taking your time with this activity and looking around your friends to get information. Once you see the new facial expressions on the Leader's face, you are copying them well. This is what friends do. When friends feel happy, their friends are happy, and when friends feel sad, their friends are sad with them."

Verbal Thinking Cues

"This is how we show empathy with our friends. This is how we recognize and take on the emotions of others. In order to share space with our friends and to show them we are thinking of them, we need to be able to show them that their feelings and mood change the way we feel."

Peer Facilitation

When a student is hurt in class, do not rush over and help the student yourself. Encourage other students to go and see what is wrong. Show concern and sadness nonverbally and use emotional language with the students you are sending to help. "Neil, I see that a friend of ours is hurt. I wonder what happened to him. I am worried about him and feel sad for him. I can't get there just yet, so could you please go over and see how he is feeling?"

Send home a description of the activity. Include these suggestions:

Start with emotion cards: i.e., pictures of children showing different feelings. Look at the picture of an emotion, copy it, and have your child copy the emotion from you. Help your child link what you are doing to an understanding of sharing emotions: "When my face was sad, you changed your face to show sadness. If a friend feels sad, that might make you feel sad too. You can show your friend that you are sad when he/she is sad."

Social Anticipation

Looking Beyond the Behavior

In a student with weak social anticipation skills, you will observe
- student has difficulty appreciating the effect of his/her behavior on another
- student has difficulty reacting in relation to others
- student does not anticipate the movements of others and understand that their movements will influence him/her

Understanding Social Anticipation Skills

Children need to move their bodies in reaction and response to another person's body. They need to anticipate what other children are doing and then know how to react in relation to them. Without this skill, the child is acting in isolation instead of interacting. In play, a child needs to be able to do more than react to the behaviors of others; he/she needs to predict and anticipate some of their behavior. Friends who get along well are often children who understand each other and have a good sense of what their friend will do, will think about, or want from a situation.

Active Skill Development

- to learn to move one's body in reaction to the movement of others

Shadow Tag

Instructions

Grades 1–6
Approximate Time: 15–30 minutes

The Shadow Hugger can receive a point each time he/she hugs a shadow, or the role of the Shadow Hugger can switch to the person whose shadow is caught. But consider playing just for the fun of the game instead of making it a competition.

1. Find a very well-lit place to play; e.g., an open field or basketball court on a sunny day.
2. Choose one student to be the Shadow Hugger. The Shadow Hugger chases the other students and tries to hug their shadows. The Shadow Hugger is not hugging the person, but the shadow, pretending to wrap his/her arms around the shadow while standing up.
3. The other students run away from the Shadow Hugger and try to keep him/her from touching their shadows.

4. You can add emotions to the game. Have students react to the contact with their shadows: e.g., when a student's shadow is hugged, that student can act happy and grateful for the hug; when someone steps on a student's shadow, that student can act disappointed and upset.

Discussion Before and After

- Discuss situations in which it is important to move your body in reaction to another.
- Reflect on how difficult it was to anticipate where a friend's body was moving at the same time as keeping track of that friend's shadow.

Moment-to-Moment Support

Zone of Proximal Development

Some children will not be very successful at this game. If a child is slow to move his/her shadow and begins to get frustrated and upset, consider modifying the game by allowing the student to move to a shaded area and hide his/her shadow when the Shadow Hugger gets close. Once you create this "safe" area, the other students will want to use it too. Allow the rest of the students five-seconds at a time in the shade, while children who need the support can stay in or near it.

Chase the Skill

Chase the interaction between the children during this game. If the children are focused on the shadows of their friends, create opportunities for them to focus their engagement on each other instead of the shadows. For example, when you hug a shadow, look to your friend and yell, "Hey, bud."

Nonverbal Cues

Guide a child's gaze awareness. Use your eyes to show him/her where he/she should be looking in order to follow the shadow successfully.

Verbal Thinking Cues

When you interact with a student who does not observe how our bodies move in relation to others, exaggerate that kind of back-and-forth. For example, if a student walks past you without noticing, exaggerate the action of stopping to say hi. If the student does not react, show how you adjust your body to move in relation to him/her by moving around his/her actions while explaining your own: "When I saw that you came into the room, I stopped what I was doing to say hi to you. Then I started to walk over to you, but we were both walking toward each other and if we kept going, we would bang into each other, so I moved over to the side so we would not hit each other."

Social Receiving

Looking Beyond the Behavior

In a student with weak social receiving skills, you will observe
- student does not consider the point of view of another
- inability to accept or see what another person needs

> Remember, treating children equally does not always mean treating them the same.

Understanding Social Receiving Skills

Children need to move their bodies as part of the group; they need to learn to be in sync with others so that they can be included. This requires cognitive flexibility. Sometimes children must resist what they want to do and match what another is doing instead. They need to be able to let go of their internal agenda and initiate and maintain a connection to the agenda of others.

Active Skill Development

- to learn to accept the needs and movements of others and to move along with them

Move Together

Instructions

Grades K–6
Approximate Time: 30 minutes

1. Collect large squares to place on the floor. You can use cardboard, carpet pieces, or garbage bags.
2. Have students line up in groups of four at one side of the room. Each group of four students has three squares.
3. Each group must work to get from one side of the room to the other, walking only on the squares. No part of their bodies can touch the ground outside the squares.

Discussion Before and After

- Discuss the benefits of teamwork and working together for a common goal.
- Reflect on the nonverbal communication tools the group used to move together.

Moment-to-Moment Support

Grouping

Consider having at least two strong personalities in each group. Do not place a less-flexible student with three adaptable peers, or the activity will be led by the child with the skill deficit. If you have an inflexible child, make sure he/she works with a student who will challenge and bring ideas, has a soft tone, and is able to manage his/her regulation.

Model

If a group of students is having trouble, go on that team yourself. Model the language they should be using to communicate and problem-solve, and demonstrate the physical risks they could take to get across the room.

Verbal Thinking Cues

"Well done, Marsha. You are being flexible with your thinking and movements. You are accepting the ideas and movements of your friends."

There are many opportunities each day to guide students peer-to-peer instead of teacher-to-student in working together for a common goal. Use every opportunity to bring peers together to perform challenging tasks under your guidance, then celebrate their teamwork, cooperation, and communication.

Space Awareness

Looking Beyond the Behavior

In a student with weak space awareness skills, you will observe
- student moves too close into another's space
- student discloses too much information

Understanding the Skill of Space Awareness

We have looked at children on the periphery of play, those who have difficulty moving with and reacting to the movements of others. But there are some children who do move with others, but move right up to them, right in their personal space. These children need physical distance reminders to help them monitor and control how they invade social space and approach too much or too quickly.

Active Skill Development

- to learn to share space with others; to move in reaction and relation to others

Octopus

Instructions

Grades K–3
Approximate Time: 15–30 minutes

1. Have students line up against a wall or fence. They are Personal Space Invaders, moving around the space.
2. Select one student to be the Personal Space Police officer. This student moves around the space, trying to touch any Personal Space Invader who comes within an arm's length of his/her body.
3. Once the Personal Space Police officer touches someone, the student who is caught sits where he/she is tagged. They join the Personal Space Police force, and help capture more Personal Space Invaders from where they are sitting by moving their arms.
4. You can add a physical cue to help students maintain an appropriate distance between themselves. Have pairs of students hold an object between them at arm's length. As they try to avoid the Personal Space Police, they also have to maintain that distance from each other.

Discussion Before and After

- Discuss which body parts (e.g., eyes, ears, brain) students need to use to concentrate while moving their bodies.

- Reflect on how hard it was for a student to stay an arm's length away from another person.

Moment-to-Moment Support

Chase the Skill

Exaggerate your nonverbal reaction to a student's physical approach. Take a big step back and mark your physical distance.

Regulate the Environment

Children who are unaware of personal space or go too close to other children do so more often when they are dysregulated. So you might see this behavior when the triggers of the environment influence a child's internal state. Pace the rhythm of the children in the room with slow music and you might notice that the child intrudes into the space of others less.

Peer Scaffolding

Show other students how to cue a student to respect their space in a kind and accepting way. Show them how they can work together to communicate as friends through this problem. For example, if Lee is too close to a peer, cue the peer to turn kindly toward Lee and gently hold both his/her hands on Lee's shoulders. He/she could say to Lee, "I like to have a little space between myself and the people I talk to. I like it when we are an arm's length apart. If it is okay with you, I will put my hands down, but this is the distance I would like us to try to keep between us." This way, you empower a peer to positively explain to a friend what he/she needs, using the "I" message and clearly explaining a skill. The peer can now support the other child with this skill, even when you are not there.

Reflective Appraisal

Looking Beyond the Behavior

In a student with weak reflective appraisal skills, you will observe
- student is aware and upset by the misbehaviors of others
- student lacks the perspective that the rules are for him/her too
- student might police the classroom and enforce rules, which he/she might not follow

Understanding Reflective Appraisal Skills

To create an accepting classroom environment, free of negative judgment, it is important to teach students to be concerned with themselves and not to worry about whether others are following the rules. This focus on a child's own behavior and not that of others empowers that child to take charge of his/her actions, while not having to be concerned with what another child should or should not do. Be sure not to use students to help you monitor the behavior of their peers. It does social damage to a child to use that child to help you enforce the rules for other children.

Active Skill Development

- to build the ability to self-monitor and focus on one's own behavior and not the behavior of others

Caught Peeking

Instructions

Grades 1–6
Approximate Time: 30 minutes

1. Students sit in a circle.
2. Calm students and avoid them getting upset by explaining that this is a game with no winners or losers. Indicate that the game is simply to prove a point; have them try to guess what the point of the game is while they play. [Game demonstrates that it is best to follow the rules and to worry about only your own behavior.]
3. Tell students that the only rule in the game is that they keep their eyes closed at all times. If they open their eyes, they are peeking. If they are caught peeking, they simply close their eyes and start again.
4. Have all students close their eyes and begin to play. Tell them, "If you catch someone peeking, call out that person's name for me."

Discussion Before and After

- Discuss how students who open their eyes to catch others peeking will get caught themselves.
- Discuss the fact that the only way to never get caught in this game is to never peek in order to catch someone else peeking.
- Discuss real-life and classroom situations in which someone concerns him/herself with someone else's behavior while breaking the rules him/herself. (Make sure no one actually names other children.)
- Reflect on what each student wanted to do in the game. Did they want to follow the no-peeking rule or did they want to catch someone else cheating in the game?

Moment-to-Moment Support

Regulate the Environment

Don't forget to monitor the children's moods during the game. If they begin to get angry or upset, pause the game and remind them of classroom expectations. A simple pause and time to breathe in a game can help to regulate and re-centre children.

Praise the Learning Process

The traditional way to play this game is that the winner is the one who catches others peeking without being caught him/herself. Games that encourage competition can be very challenging for children who struggle with winning and losing. In contrast, this game has been altered to help children focus on what is important in games: to monitor their own behavior. As you play this game, reward the children who never open their eyes. They are the ones who will never get caught cheating. These are the children who followed the rules and are worried about only their own behavior.

Reward System

In class, students should be rewarded for helping their friends, not for getting their friends in trouble. Help students distinguish between getting someone in trouble and getting someone out of trouble. If their actions hurt the person who was misbehaving, then they are simply trying to get that person in trouble. If the actions prevent someone or something from being hurt, then they got that person out of trouble; this behavior should be reinforced with some sort of reward. Also consider rewarding students when they tell you or someone else of a great thing that another child did. For example, "Thanks for telling me that Jenny had a great idea. Put a token in the jar for sharing your group's successes."

Sometimes you have to weigh which skill deficit is more important for you to address; for example, Lee not sitting still or Neil's negative focus on the behavior of his peers. Try to reward Neil for helping Lee calm down, instead of for telling on Lee.

5

Actively Developing Emotional Skills

Expressing Emotions

Looking Beyond the Behavior

In a student with weak skills of expressing emotions, you will observe
- student is unaware of how he/she reacts to his/her own emotions
- student has an inflated emotional reaction without understanding what it looks like to others

Understanding Expressive Emotions Skills

We are only examining the emotions, not placing a value judgment on them. For example, for some children, walking into the classroom is stressful. We want to allow children to examine their emotions, not tell them that it is not a big deal to go to school, that everyone does it.

Some children need help identifying what emotions look like, in others as well as themselves. These children might have large reactions but be unaware what they look like when they exhibit these reactions. We must help them examine their emotions. Then they need help looking at how they present these emotions to others. This expression of emotion needs to be examined separately from the validity of their reaction to the problem. When children who hyper-react to a problem are simultaneously told to calm down and that they should not be upset about what they are upset about, we are combining two separate issues. First, examine with the child what he/she looks like when he/she is very upset. Separately, examine which issues are more socially acceptable to get very upset about.

Active Skill Development

- to learn how to communicate emotions to others

Emotions Look Like

Instructions

Grades K–3
Approximate Time: 30–45 minutes

1. Make sure each student has cut-out paper circles or a sheet of paper with circles drawn on it
2. Explain that feelings come from what we think and how our bodies feel. Explain that we are able to show those thoughts and feelings in our faces.
3. Label each circle with an emotion. Have students draw what they think a face experiencing that emotion would look like. Encourage and praise. Do not correct. Learn from the drawings.

4. Expand this activity by making a Mood Continuum. On a large piece of paper (from a roll of brown kraft paper), write *MY FACE LOOKS ANGRY* on the far left side, and *MY FACE LOOKS HAPPY* on the far right side.
5. Make a list of extreme emotions: e.g., *delighted, overjoyed, wonderful, blissful, devastated, depressed, annoyed, furious, livid*. Have students show what they think their faces would look like for each emotion.
6. Draw or photograph facial expressions to go with each emotion and label the expression on the face with the emotion. Decide together where each emotion belongs on the Mood Continuum.
7. Look at the faces on the right side. Discuss how our faces feel and look when we are positive and energized. Look at the faces on the left side. Discuss how our faces feel and look when we feel negative emotions.
8. Discuss the gap between the extremes where there are no emotions. Make a list of more moderate emotions: e.g., *good, okay, calm, content, glad, unsure, relaxed, upset, sad, disappointed, frustrated*. Again, act out each emotion, create a face for it, and place it on the Mood Continuum.
9. Look at the faces in the middle of the line. Discuss moderate emotions and how they are less taxing on our energy systems.

Discussion Before and After

- Discuss what particular emotions mean to students.
- Reflect on a time when a student felt the feeling and what it meant to him/her.

Moment-to-Moment Support

Model

Consistently provide models about how mood and facial appearance are related. For example, "My eyes just got big and I am glaring. My mouth is tight and scowling. I am upset."; "I am crying and looking down at the floor because I feel sad."

Verbal Thinking Cues

"I think you are sending me a message with the look on your face. I see that your eyes look like they are shining, your smile extends to each side of your face, and you are laughing. You are showing me with your face that you are happy."

Chase the Skill

Exaggerate your facial reactions to situations. This can be done every time you read a story to the class. Mimic the faces of the characters in the story and discuss why the faces would look the way they do.

Nonverbal Cues

Place the Mood Continuum in the classroom and point to it during the day.

Detailed Positive Praise

Label the emotion and praise the child's ability to cope with it anytime his/her body or emotion appears moderate. For example: "Cool, Neil. At first your body looked tense in the basketball game. It seemed to me that you shrugged it off, like it was only a little frustrating and no big deal. I am very proud of you. It looked like you were beginning to think that there was a problem, but then you walked back to your team and laughed with your group. That kept you from getting caught up in the problem and getting more upset."

Peer Facilitation

Take extreme care to avoid helping one child summarize why he/she is mad at another child and what that child did that upset him/her. Try not to facilitate a dialogue that has a child telling another what he/she did wrong. Instead, try to help each child reflect on his/her own behavior, contribution to the problem, and possible escalation of the event. Encourage the child to stick with the "I" message of how he/she feels in the situation: for example, "I wish I had not hit you when you took my toy."

Homework

Send home a description of the activity. Include these suggestions:

> If your child struggles to understand the nonverbal cues of facial expressions, you can support him/her at home by cutting out pictures of kids' emotional faces. With your child, look at them, play games with them (e.g., a Concentration-type matching game to match different faces with the same emotion). Post the faces in a room that you have fun in, so that they are available to look at and discuss.

Neil

Neil seems to respond in mood extremes. If the only moods he feels are elated and devastated, that will affect his behavior. He needs help understanding his mood vocabulary and expanding it (see chart on page 124).

Internalizing Emotions

Looking Beyond the Behavior

In a student with weak skills of internalizing emotions, you will observe
- student does not understand the different physical sensations emotions create in the body
- student confuses one emotion for another.

Understanding the Skills of Internalizing Emotions

Children with emotional-regulation challenges struggle to appropriately link the body's sensations with an emotion. They misinterpret neurophysiological responses, such as muscle tension, light-headedness, stomach pains, flushed face, racing heart. All young children cry when they are tired or get very grumpy when they are hungry; as they age, most learn to recognize the connection between their physical and emotional states. But some children are very slow to gain this physical awareness of their own bodies; e.g., they do not recognize that their stomach-ache, headache, or racing heart is because there is a spelling test. We can help children make more connections between how their body is reacting and the causes of those feelings, external and internal.

Active Skill Development

- to practice linking the body's internal sensations with an emotional vocabulary

Emotions Feel Like…

Instructions

Grades K–3
Approximate Time: 30–45 minutes

1. Have each student lie down and trace his/her full body on large piece of paper to create a body map.
2. Explain, "We feel our feelings throughout our bodies. Let's draw where we feel different emotions."
3. Do one feeling together as a class. Pick a feeling you have already talked about, perhaps one that underlies some of your particular classroom challenges (for example, jealousy). Have students close their eyes and think about the place in their bodies they feel that feeling.
4. Pick a corresponding feeling color (see chart below) and have students color in that place on the body map. Use different shades of the same color for related emotions to show the connection; for example, anger and annoyance are two shades of red.

Basic Emotions	Expanded Emotional Vocabulary
Happy: yellow	Satisfied: light yellow
Disgusted: grey	Repulsed: dark grey
Surprised: black	Shocked: black with black outline
Worried: orange	Nervous: light orange
Angry: red	Annoyed: light red
Sad: blue	Depressed: deep blue

Encourage and praise. Do not correct. Learn from your students' responses and drawings.

5. Pick one emotion at a time and examine it.

SAMPLE EXAMINATION OF ANGER

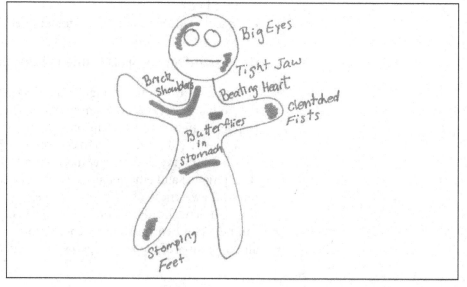

6. Make a small stick figure for each emotion and add it to the Mood Continuum (see page 108).

Discussion Before and After

- Discuss what impact feelings have on the body.
- Reflect on a time a student's body hurt or felt tired because of feelings; help him/her think about a time he/she felt energized and great after having positive emotions.

Moment-to-Moment Support

Model

When you are teaching, show students your frustration when you can't solve a math problem. Then show them the tightness in your shoulders that you feel from the frustration. Show them how you stretch your arms to relieve the tension and help yourself stay calm.

Scaffolding

Support a child by helping him/her deconstruct his/her internal feelings and his/her emotions. For example, explain that a trigger makes the child nervous or upset, so the brain sends a danger message throughout the child's body, making his/her stomach hurt, heart beat faster, and shoulders tense.

Homework

Send home a description of the activity. Include these suggestions:

> Place a large cutout of your child's body in a main area of the house. Consistently label body parts and isolate where in the body your child feels his/her stress. You might consider starting to model relaxation techniques to show your child how you calm physical stress, tensing and relaxing different muscles in the body.

Externalizing Emotions

Looking Beyond the Behavior

When dealing with meltdowns (see Chapter 7 for more), it is important to realize that there are two separate issues: the cause of the emotional dysregulation (the reason for the meltdown) and the behavior the child engages in as he/she dysregulates (what the child does during the meltdown).

In a student with weak skills of externalizing emotions, you will observe
- student does not link positive or negative emotions to the physical sensations in the body and his/her reactionary behavior
- lack of understanding that behavioral reactions are not socially acceptable
- student reacts in the moment to his/her own extreme negative feelings

Understanding the Skills of Externalizing Emotions

Children with emotional-regulation challenges get into trouble when their extreme moods make them react inappropriately. If we can help them link their moods to their behavior, we can help them understand the power their moods have over them. We can help them see that they can feel angry, but they can't act angry; it is the action that gets them in trouble.

Active Skill Development

- to learn that there is a connection between the way we feel and the way we act

Emotions Act Like...

Instructions

Grades K–3
Approximate Time: 30–45 minutes

Throughout this book, shapes are used to show emotions and actions:

♡ Heart = what we feel

▭ Rectangle = what we do

🗩 Speech balloon = what we say

🗨 Thought bubble = what we think

1. Find a clear area with lots of space.
2. Post the Mood Continuum (see page 108) where all students can see it.
3. Pick one emotion and display a picture of the emotion. Ask students to close their eyes and think about what they might do when they feel this emotion. For example, a student might say that when he is angry, he yells.
4. Write the action verb on a large, rectangular piece of paper. It is important to use a rectangle to represent physical action.
5. Place the rectangle on the Mood Continuum just under the emotion.
6. Continue through the emotions, linking them with actions and posting them on the Mood Continuum.
7. After completing this activity, you can continue to add to the Mood Continuum. Whenever you see behavior linked to a mood, take a minute to write down the negative action and place it with the corresponding emotion.

Discussion Before and After

- Discuss how negative emotions correspond with negative behavior, and positive emotions correspond with positive behavior.
- Reflect on a time you did something you are not proud of because you were angry.

Moment-to-Moment Support

Nonverbal Cues

It is important to help students understand that, in periods of stress, the most important way they can help themselves is to stop talking. Instead of entering a child's personal space and telling him/her to calm down and relax, develop specific signals that indicate that the child's hands should be at his/her side and that he/she should stop talking. Help him/her move away from verbal and cognitive interaction and into a sensory break.

Verbal Thinking Cue

Not at the moment of dysregulation, but when the child is calm, help him/her understand the impact of his/her dysregulation. "Most often, we do not get in trouble for what we are upset about, we get in trouble for the way we react when we are upset. If we are able to manage the way we react when we are upset, then other people might be more interested in listening to our thoughts and opinions about what got us upset in the first place."

Proactive Explanation

"I hear what you are upset about and we can talk about that later. For now, what worries me is the way you are reacting while you are upset. Let's slow down first and take a break. You can feel sad, mad, and upset, but you can't push, shove, and punch. Let's calm down together."

Emotional Regulation

Looking Beyond the Behavior

In a student with weak emotional regulation skills, you will observe
- student gets very upset and is unable to calm down
- student is not aware that the tools used to calm our bodies when energized can be used when we are upset

Understanding Emotional Regulation Skills

Children with emotional-regulation challenges have trouble self-regulating when their emotions take over their thinking. We can empower them to understand that they can identify tools that are effective for calming their body's emotional stress. We can help support children with these tools by using them proactively when we see children beginning to be upset and by allowing them a physical space where they can calm themselves down.

Active Skill Development

- to learn to identify, understand, monitor, and manage appropriate moods and emotions
- to learn to match one's mood to the demands of the situation or environment

I Know What Tool to Use

Instructions

Grades 1–6
Approximate Time: 15–45 minutes

1. Refer to the list of tools from Tools for Cool on page 59. Draw pictures of the tools and label them with the action.
2. As a class, brainstorm which areas of the body each tool would help; for example, yoga would help tense shoulders.
3. Look at the body maps from Emotions Feel Like… on page 110. Write the tools on sticky notes and attach them to the areas of the body they help regulate.

Discussion Before and After

- Discuss how a particular tool works well with specific areas of the body.
- Reflect on whether the child will be able to use the tool in the moment; i.e., when upset.

Moment-to-Moment Support

Regulate the Environment

Provide sensory breaks during an activity if you see that a student is beginning to get upset. Include the whole group by pausing the game and having all the students sit down, or support one student by calling him/her over—not to discipline, but to distract. For example, with a smile on your face, call out, "Neil, I need to ask you something." You might ask a question about a favorite cartoon. As you develop a supportive relationship with your student, he/she will begin to understand why you are calling him/her over.

Scaffolding

If you know which calming technique helps a student when he/she is upset, don't tell him/her to do it; instead, do it for or with the student. For example, if humor helps the child, do not tell him/her to make a joke, but be ready to say or do something silly to help distract him/her; if looking away helps the child, do not tell him/her to look away, but come gently into his/her space, move between him/her and the trigger, then try to point the child to look away.

Homework

Send home a description of the activity. Include these suggestions:

> In order to help your child use tools under stress (i.e., when environmental demands exceed his/her skills), you must consistently reinforce the strategies during calm and non-stressful situations. In your daily life, discuss how you self-calm yourself, and examine which strategies help him/her remain calm. Link your emotional stress to your coping technique. "I am starting to feel frustrated right now, so I am going to take a break and close my eyes. I just need to stop thinking about this problem and let my body relax." Discuss the benefits of various tools and the situations in which they might be used. If you try to teach your child these strategies when he/she is upset, he/she may not be willing or able to try them.

Emotional Modulation

Looking Beyond the Behavior

In a student with weak emotional behavior skills, you will observe
- student reacts to small problems in big ways
- student has extreme reactions to problems
- student's view of what is and is not a big problem differs from that of most people

Understanding Emotional Modulation Skills

Children with emotional-modulation difficulties have a hard time matching their reaction to the seriousness of a problem. Any challenge, disagreement, or issue feels like a huge problem to them. It is important to understand that some children physically experience acute anxiety over issues that do not upset most people. If you dismiss the importance they place on a problem or undermine their feelings, you will not help the child begin to understand how his/her over-reaction to small problems affects him/herself and others. We can help children cognitively evaluate their problems and assess the challenges they are having extreme reactions to.

Active Skill Development

- to learn to emotionally rate the seriousness of environmental triggers or problems and to react accordingly

How Big Is that Problem?

Instructions

Grades 1–3
Approximate Time: 30–45 minutes

1. Create a Problem Continuum on a large piece of paper. On the far left side, write HUGE PROBLEM. Moving to the other side of the paper, write *BIG PROBLEM, LITTLE PROBLEM, NOT A PROBLEM.*
2. Read aloud a rectangular Scenario Card from page 116. Discuss the situation with students.
3. As a class, decide how big a problem it is. Agree on a place for it on the Problem Continuum.
4. Try not to correct or judge. Mark everything on the line. Once you are done, review it as a class. Sometimes, children readjust the seriousness of certain problem by seeing it in relation to others.
5. Discuss positive self-talk you could use to help you in the situation. For example: "Too bad, because I have a lot of fun playing with my friend. Maybe I can ask if we can have another playdate soon." You can write the self-talk in a speech balloon and attach it to the scenario card.
6. Have students write their own scenarios and make their own charts. It is important for students to assess how their perception of problems might differ from that of others. But emphasize that you are simply plotting the problems, not judging the validity of them.

To use this in conjunction with the Mood Continuum (see page 108), your paper should be half as long as the one for the Mood Continuum, because it is limited to the negative emotions. Once a problem is placed on the Problem Continuum, discuss if the problem matches the seriousness of the mood on the Mood Continuum.

See page 116 for Scenario Cards.

Discussion Before and After

- Discuss with students how their bodies felt when they thought about a *BIG PROBLEM.*
- Discuss how they feel about knowing some self-talk strategies to calm themselves down.
- Reflect on how hard each student thinks it is to calm down from a *BIG PROBLEM.*

Moment-to-Moment Support

Zone of Proximal Development

Some children are not able to do this. The very child this activity would be of most benefit to will be the one who might not be able to accept changing his/her mind about the seriousness of the problem. But this activity is an important opportunity for you to understand the mindframe of some of the children in your class. You will not help a cognitively inflexible child change his/her mind

Scenario Cards

Your mom tells you that you can't have ice cream.	You lose a card game.	Your friend does not want to play your game.
There are only blue cups, not pink ones, to drink from.	Your pet fish died.	You friend is mad at you because you lost her book.
You are allowed to watch only one TV show before bed.	Your friend took the book you wanted out of the library.	Your friend rolled a higher number, so he gets to go first.
Your friend has the same Halloween costume as you.	Your dad says it's going to rain all weekend so he has to cancel the camping trip.	Your sister went into your room and messed up all your books.
Your friend said that your coat is old and ugly.	You see someone making fun of your brother.	You didn't finish your homework, so you don't get to go out for recess.
You are allowed only one piece of cake for dessert.	There's a movie you really want to watch, but it's your sister's turn to pick.	Your dad didn't get to the store, so there are no waffles for breakfast.
You have to miss a play-date because you have to go to the dentist after school.	Your brother gets to go to a birthday party, but you were not invited.	It is bath time, so you need to go upstairs.
You lost your hat at school.	You fell and broke your ankle, so you won't be able to play outside games for two months.	Your family is moving to another city.
Your friends all went to a party and did not invite you.	Your friend is a better swimmer than you.	Your mom tells you to clean your room.

© 2013 *Moment by Moment* by Joey Mandel. Pembroke Publishers. ISBN 978-1-55138-287-6.

on the seriousness of a problem by saying it is not that serious a problem. Accept that the child is rating the seriousness of the problems according to his/her world view, and you will better understand the issues with which this child needs support.

Model

Demonstrate problem assessment with your own reactions. For example, get really upset when something small happens: "Oh no, my pencil fell on the ground! This is a huge problem." Warn students before you do this if you think they might be overwhelmed by your reaction.

Reward System

In an ability-based reward system, a child can be rewarded for being flexible and for remaining emotionally calm in a situation or in the face of a trigger that, at his/her developmental age, should not upset him/her. It is okay to reward a child for social behaviors that all of his/her peers do with ease. For example, if a child indicated that not wearing red on Tuesday was a *HUGE PROBLEM* and had always worn red on Tuesday, then he/she should be rewarded any time he/she is wearing any other colors on Tuesday.

Understanding the Skill Deficit

For some students, anxiety underlies much of their behavior. In order to help these students, maintain a pattern of 10% empathy first, then 90% exposure to the anxiety-causing situation. Your interaction needs start with the understanding that you know that the task is very hard for him/her, but try not to give a lot of positive attention or rewards when a student is in a state of anxiety. Your body language should be neutral and you should not engage too much. Your empathetic acknowledgment could be a simple head nod and a kind look. If you use verbal language, it should acknowledge how the child feels and then give the child proactive steps to help him/herself: "Good morning, Marsha. I see that it has been a hard morning for you to come to school. I am proud that you are here. Great work. Go get a book and read at your desk, doing some slow breathing to help distract your mind and slow down your heartbeat."

Tone Modulation

Looking Beyond the Behavior

In a student with weak tone modulation skills, you will observe
- student expresses negative emotion when speaking with others
- negative emotion is verbally expressed

Understanding Tone Modulation Skills

Children can be unaware of the impact their body language and tone of voice have on the message they are sending. We need to demonstrate for them the effect of their tone and have them practice emotional body language. Too often, we correct children being verbally rude by using rude verbal and nonverbal behavior ourselves. We must help children see what using a harsh tone of voice looks like and sounds like in order to motivate them to want to self-monitor their own tone.

Active Skill Development

- to learn to manage emotional expression

Changing the Tone of the Conversation

Instructions

Grades K–6
Approximate Time: 15 minutes

1. Start with students sitting in a circle or at their desks.
2. Choose an Emotional Mismatch card from page 119. Tell students the emotion and point to the emotion on the Mood Continuum (see page 108).
3. Have students read the sentence as a group in the emotional tone. Repeat a few times.
4. Divide the class into two groups; separate the groups by a little distance.

Students can add nonverbal actions when they say the sentence.

5. Begin with the first group whispering the line. Then signal the other group to say the same line a little louder.
6. Have the first group say the line a little louder. Continue switching back and forth between groups while increasing the volume.
7. Help students maintain the same emotion and tone no matter what the volume of their voices.
8. Use the Say It Like This chart below to have students say one sentence in multiple emotional tones.
9. Have students do the same activity with sentences of your choice.

This part of the activity can be done as a choral round: divide students into two groups; have the first group start to say the sentence; the second group starts before the first group is finished the sentence.

SAMPLE OF SAY IT LIKE THIS

Sentence	Emotional Tone	
I don't like it when you grab my toy.	Loud	Calm
	Soft	Sing
	Scream	Cry
	Screech	
No, I don't want to play that.	Loud	Calm
	Soft	Sing
	Scream	Cry
	Screech	
Can I have another one?	Loud	Calm
	Soft	Sing
	Scream	Cry
	Screech	

Discussion Before and After

- Discuss the way you feel when a friend uses a harsh tone or yells at you.
- Reflect on a time when you were not angry, but someone thought you were because of the way you spoke with him/her.

Emotional Mismatch

(Depressed)
She is so funny. I love hanging out with her and spending time with her. She cracks me up.

(Anxious)
I just got another Wii game. I am so lucky.

(Joyful)
I failed my math test because I did not study.

(Furious)
Do you want to come over to my house for a playdate?

(Surprised)
I am so tired, I need to go to bed.

(Guilty)
Here, you can have half my sandwich.

(Shy)
I am a fantastic hockey player.

© 2013 *Moment by Moment* by Joey Mandel. Pembroke Publishers. ISBN 978-1-55138-287-6.

Moment-to-Moment Support

Grouping

This is a whole-class heterogenous activity. All students can participate in this activity as a group.

Scaffolding

Some children might need time to practice the emotion first. Let the student go into the hall or have the class close their eyes so that they can't see him/her practice.

Verbal Thinking Cue

"This is confusing. Your words are telling me something, but your body is telling me something else."

Model

Show students the impact their tone of voice has on you. Exaggerate your facial look of confusion, or your hurt feelings from a sharp response.

Paraphrase

Some children use harsh tones of voice and harsh words during social conversations with their peers. If your reaction to their emotional extremes is to discipline them and react harshly, you will be showing them the negative response their dysregulation elicits. If you yell at a child for being rude, you will not show that child how to speak with softness and kindness. Instead, paraphrase the child's sentence in a soft and gentle way.

Neil

Neil's harsh tone is the beginning of his dysregulation. Helping him learn to manage his tone will be a first step in helping him manage his emotional escalation.

- Model a soft tone.
- When he uses a harsh tone, repeat in a soft tone.
- Do not judge or correct his tone, especially with a harsh voice.
- When he uses a soft tone, praise him in detail.
- Link his ability to repeat the sentence in a soft voice to his ability to calm himself.

Optimistic Thinking

Looking Beyond the Behavior

In a student with weak optimistic thinking skills, you will observe
- student interprets every situation in a negative way
- student thinks about a situation from a negative viewpoint

Understanding Optimistic Thinking Skills

The basis of Cognitive Behavior Therapy is that if we change the way we think, we can change the way we feel. Children need to be shown different ways to think about a situation.

Active Skill Development

- to learn to recognize that we can positively influence our thinking, which will in turn change the way we feel and act

Thinking Makes It So

Instructions

Grades 1–6
Approximate Time: 30–45 minutes

1. Hand out paper circles to the students.
2. Have them draw a face on each circle to represent a different emotion: e.g., happy, jealous, angry, guilty, worried, sympathetic, sad, embarrassed, irritated, proud, caring, excited.
3. Read out a situation and a thought process from the How You Think Means How You Feel chart on page 122. Students hold up the face that represents the mood they would feel if they thought in that way.
4. Have students come up with their own examples.

Throughout this book, shapes are used to show emotions and actions:

Heart = what we feel

Rectangle = what we do

Speech balloon = what we say

Thought bubble = what we think

Discussion Before and After

- Discuss how having a different thought will affect how they feel.
- Reflect on how they felt in each situation.

Moment-to-Moment Support

Regulate the Environment

Set up students on mats and have them act out the situations.

Chase the Skill

If you have a child in your class who seems depressed, disparaging, and negative in his/her thoughts, this activity can help that student understand that positive thoughts can make positive changes.

Self Talk

Consistently label your thinking with emotions. Try to use examples that echo the issues and struggles students face in your classroom, but not identify individual students. For example, if your students often misinterpret the intentions of their friends, provide an example of misinterpreting the intentions of other teachers, using an example that has nothing to do with the actual event: "I wanted to volunteer to be track-and-field coach this year. I was really excited about it and had some great ideas. But when I went to sign up, another teacher had already signed up for it. Everyone always does this to me. They take what I want on purpose. It is not fair." Examine the validity of this type of thinking with students; they will likely be very good at helping you see that you are wrong. Help them list examples of similar misinterpretations they might make.

How You Think Means How You Feel

Situation	Thoughts
You have to finish your homework assignment in class, so you go outside late for recess. By the time you get outside, your two friends are playing together in the sand pit without you.	It looks like they are having a lot of fun without me. I bet they do not want me to come over and play.
	Great, it looks like they are having fun. I can't wait to play.
	It looks like they are laughing. I wonder if they are talking about me.
Sally walks over to your group and looks angry and mad.	Oh, no. I wonder what is upsetting her. She is normally so happy.
	Sally looks really mad at me. She must be upset because three days ago I walked home without her.
	Sally is always crying and upset about something.
You are talking with a friend, but he never looks you in the eyes. He always looks away.	Is he bored with my conversation? He must not like me.
	I think it is hard for my friend to look me in the eyes while he is talking. I will just keep talking and try not to get distracted when he looks away.
	Why does he keep looking away? Does he have something to hide or is he just being rude to me?
Your mom goes out for dinner with her friends	That's okay. Mom likes to have a nice dinner out, but she always comes back and I see her in the morning. I am going to look into my toolbox to find a strategy to calm my racing heart.
	If Mom leaves the house, something bad could happen. Then I will feel sad and alone.
	It is not fair that Mom goes out with her friends instead of with me. She likes them more than she likes me.
Every time you explain something to your friend, he speaks at the same time as you and says, "Yes I know, yes I know, yes I know."	He thinks I am saying something boring that he already knows. I guess I should stop talking because I have nothing important to say.
	What I say has such great value that my friend agrees with everything I say. We think along the exact same lines.
	I love this friend of mine. He is a wonderful person who has many strengths. He does struggle a little when it comes to the way he interacts with people. He interrupts a little when people talk, but he is not trying to be rude, he just speaks with people a little differently than I do. No big deal.

© 2013 *Moment by Moment* by Joey Mandel. Pembroke Publishers. ISBN 978-1-55138-287-6.

Positive Affect

Looking Beyond the Behavior

In a student with weak positive affect skills, you will observe
- student does not seem to understand that other children have feelings too
- student does not understand that his/her moods change the moods of others

Understanding Positive Affect Skills

Do not assume that a child is being mean on purpose. Often children are unaware of the impact of their moods on others. Help them see the connection of their mood to the moods of others.

Children need to understand that emotions are transferable. It is important that they recognize that their behavior and mood have an impact on the people with whom they share space. Their rough hello when they walk into the class is greeted by rough hellos back, and a whole negative cycle begins.

Active Skill Development

- to learn that we can positively influence the way others feel

I Can Change How You Feel

Instructions

Grades K–6
Approximate Time: 15 minutes

1. Pick two students to stand at opposite ends of the classroom or hallway. One student is Mood Influencer; the other is the Mood Taker.
2. The Mood Influencer will not change his/her demeanor during the whole activity. The Mood Taker's job is to change his/her demeanor to copy that of the Mood Influencer.
3. Give both students emotions to act out. Each student is given a different emotion.
4. Students walk toward each other, each acting out the emotion word on their own card. Once they are close, the Mood Taker must change from his/her emotion to that of the Mood Influencer.
5. Once students get used to this game, they can start to choose their own emotions.
6. After using the basic moods, expand students' emotional vocabulary by using the chart on page 124.

Encourage as much nonverbal body language as possible.

Discussion Before and After

- Discuss the impact of other people being able to change our moods at school and at home.
- Reflect on a time that the mood of someone else changed their mood.

Moment-to-Moment Support

Structure

To make this activity easier, have partners sit across from each other in two lines. Point to the partners from the first line. Give the same emotion to each whole

Emotion Words

Energized	Confused	Pleased	Apathetic	Elated
Angry	Depressed	Content	Satisfied	Confident
Frustrated	Melancholy	Worried	Relaxed	Joyful
Irritated	Sad	Insecure	Calm	Happy
Enraged	Silly	Chilled	Bored	Ecstatic
Upset	Disappointed	Optimistic	Bitter	Anxious
Afraid	Panicked	Disapproving	Astounded	Displeased
Merry	Super	Okay	Good	Jumpy
Determined	Lonely	Indifferent	Pained	Relieved
Hurt	Frightened	Curious	Concentrating	Cautious
Alienated	Aggressive	Humiliated	Exhausted	Miserable
Disgusted	Interested	Hysterical	Mischievous	Undecided
Surprised	Nervous	Thrilled	Jealous	Devastated
Unsure	Puzzled	Sheepish	Stubborn	Hostile
Excited	Furious	Upset	Gloomy	Delighted
Sleepy	Withdrawn	Negative	Thoughtful	Shy
Stressed	Guilty	Puzzled	Regretful	Suspicious
Livid	Ashamed	Concerned	Proud	Bashful
Embarrassed	Jubilant			

© 2013 *Moment by Moment* by Joey Mandel. Pembroke Publishers. ISBN 978-1-55138-287-6.

line of children. Have one line change from their given emotion to that of the other line. Practice this in the lines with different emotions before acting it out one at a time.

Verbal Thinking Cue

"If we are in a bad mood and are rude to our friends, it affects the way they feel in general and the way they feel about us. We want to be careful with our moods and our words around our friends, so that we don't change the way they feel in a negative way. If I know that I can change the way my friend feels, should I try to help my friend feel happy or sad?"

Detailed Positive Praise

Consistently detail the impact of students' positive moods on their friends: "Wow, the class sure is happy right now. It is wonderful to be in an environment of smiles and laughter." Do not use this strategy in periods of meltdown, detailing the impact of negative emotions on others. It will make the student more upset and/or guilty and will escalate the negative reaction.

Model

Model your own awareness of your negative emotions and their impact on others. Some students hyper-react to negative emotions, and their negative behavior increases in severity as your emotions escalate. Be willing to recognize this and discuss it. For example, Lee's dysregulation is affected by negative reactions to his behavior. He can sense dislike for his behavior and, instead of using it to control his behavior, he might engage in more and more inappropriate behavior because he senses the teacher's disapproval.

Homework

Send home a description of the activity. Include these suggestions:

> Your child might need a little extra help recognizing emotions in other people and him/herself. Be sure to practice the activity first, maintaining the emotions and pairing a visual representation of the emotion with a real-life face. Make exaggerated face drawings that show a face with the emotion. Bring the drawn face up to your face, have your child focus on your face making the same emotion, then bring the drawn face back to your face. Give your child his own face with the same emotion as yours and repeat the actions together. Once your child understands these emotions, place all the drawn faces on his/her side. Each time you show an emotion in your face, have your child find the emotion on the drawn faces and bring it up to his/her face.

Emotional Agency

Looking Beyond the Behavior

In a student with weak skills of emotional agency, you will observe
- student does not make the link between behavior and how he/she feels
- student does not understand that his/her actions have emotional impact on him/herself and others

Understanding the Skills of Receptive Emotional Agency

Other people have the power to change our moods. This affects how our minds and bodies feel. Children can build an awareness of how other people's actions can change their mood and affect how their bodies feel. By examining this relationship through both positive and negative feelings, children can be motivated to take more ownership of their reaction to the environmental triggers that upset them and those around them.

Active Skill Development

- to learn that positive and negative behavior influences how people feel

How We Act Affects How We Feel

Instructions

Grades K–6
Approximate Time: 30 minutes

1. Remind students of the different emotions and how you have been exploring them together.
2. Have students spread out around the room. Tell them they can close their eyes if they wish.
3. Read out questions from the How Do I Feel When… chart below. Ask students to strike the emotion pose they feel reflects the question.

These questions involve receptive emotional agency; i.e., that the actions of others can change how we feel.

HOW DO I FEEL WHEN...

- How do I feel when someone says hi to me?
- How do I feel when someone hits me?
- How do I feel when someone smiles at me?
- How do I feel when someone yells at me?
- How do I feel when someone wants to sit beside me?
- How do I feel when someone interrupts me?
- How do I feel when someone reads a book with me?
- How do I feel when someone shares his/her snack with me?
- How do I feel when someone colors with me?
- How do I feel when someone laughs with me?
- How do I feel when someone says I can't play?
- How do I feel when we walk into the gym?
- How I feel when the teacher is in a bad mood?
- How do I feel when someone takes my toy?
- How do I feel when someone laughs at me?
- How do I feel when someone says something I don't understand?
- How do I feel when someone ignores me?
- How do I feel when someone talks only about him/herself?
- How do I feel when someone stands too close?
- How do I feel when someone does not listen to me?
- How do I feel when someone asks nice questions about me?
- How do I feel when someone lets me take my turn first?
- How do I feel when someone breaks my stuff?
- How do I feel when someone asks me how I am feeling?
- How do I feel when the class is noisy?
- How do I feel when my good friend is not at school?

4. Use language to discuss their poses and those of their friends; for example, "Would you call that embarrassed or upset?"
5. Repeat the activity with questions from the How Do Others Feel When I... chart.

These questions involve expressive emotional agency; i.e., that our own actions can change how other people feel.

HOW DO OTHERS FEEL WHEN I...

- How does your mom feel when you do the dishes?
- How does your mom feel when you hit your brother?
- How does your mom feel when your teacher says you did well at school?
- How does your mom feel when you say a bad word?
- How does your mom feel when you eat your whole dinner?
- How does your dad feel when you play ball with him?
- How does your dad feel when you scream and shout?
- How does your dad feel when you mess up the basement?
- How does your grandma feel when you listen to her while she reads to you?
- How does your grandma feel when you turn your back on her?
- How does your grandma feel when you interrupt her when she is talking?
- How does your classmate feel when you call him/her stupid?
- How does your classmate feel when you tell him/her you don't like him?
- How does your dad feel when you tell him about your day?
- How does your dad feel when you cry while he is helping you with your homework?
- How does your friend feel when you tell him/her you had fun playing with him/her?
- How does your friend feel when you will play only the games you want?
- How does your friend feel when you agree to play by his/her rules?
- How does your sister feel when you will not let her play with you and your friends?
- How does your sister feel when you make fun of her?
- How does your brother feel when you tell him he looks funny?
- How does your teacher feel when you sit in your desk during the lesson?
- How does your teacher feel when you do your homework?
- How does your grandpa feel when you talk only about yourself and don't ask him any questions?
- How does your classmate feel when you tell other kids to stop talking to him?
- How do the kids you're playing with feel when you start to yell and scream in anger?

Discussion Before and After

- Discuss the difference between the way the body feels after kind and unkind actions.
- Reflect on how students feel in their bodies (e.g., arms, legs, heart) after someone does something nice to them. Then reflect on how they felt when someone does something not so nice.

Moment-to-Moment Support

Regulate the Environment

If your class cannot handle the unpredictable movement and energy of this activity, have students sit at their desks with cutouts of happy and sad faces. They can raise the happy face to represent a positive effect or a sad face to represent a negative effect.

Verbal Thinking Cue

"If we have a better understanding of the reasons we feel happy or angry, then we will have more thinking and feeling options to help us calm ourselves."

Chase the Skills

Consistently talk about feelings and their impact on the body, the thinking, and then the behavior choices of students. Do not tell students what they are thinking and feeling, but help them make links and connections in the moment.

Detailed Positive Praise

Praise positive feelings while explaining the impact of an event on the way a student feels: "Marsha, you seem very happy right now. I saw that your friend was just kind to you and helped you. I wonder if you are smiling and happy right now because of that."

Homework

Send home a description of the activity. Include these suggestions:

> Make lists with your child of all the things that make you feel happy and all the things that make you feel sad. Each make your own lists. Think about the issues you will choose to model for your child. They should be real issues of your own, but they should be things he/she can relate to. For example, you could write that you have a colleague at work you struggle to get along with; or, if your child is afraid of dogs, you could list something you are afraid of. Sit down with your child and pick one issue each that you think you would like to work on being able to better handle.

Emotional Liability

Looking Beyond the Behavior

In a student with weak emotional liability skills, you will observe
- student does not understand that others have challenges and struggles too
- student does not see the emotional perspective of others

Understanding Emotional Liability Skills

Our actions have emotional consequences for other people. It is important to help children consider the chain of events of which they are a part and to consider the people with whom they share space as having strengths and challenges. Social acceptance and forgiveness begins with understanding the situation from the other person's point of view, not just our own. If we see each social dilemma only from our own point of view, it is hard to compromise or solve problems collaboratively. As adults, we can support children by consistently helping them consider the point of view of the other person, as well as the impact of our behavior on him/her.

Active Skill Development

- to develop the ability to understand the emotional perspective of others

If You Knew

Instructions

Grades 1–6
Approximate Time: 30 minutes

1. Have students lie back and close their eyes. Tell them you will ask them some questions.
2. Read out the If You Knew… questions from the table below, one at a time.

IF YOU KNEW…

If you knew that the boy you made fun of at school went home and cried all night because of you, would you act differently?	If you knew that when you said, "I don't want to be in his group" the boy felt devastated, would you act differently?
If you knew that when you told everyone at school "Jenny is annoying" that she heard you and started to cry, would you act differently?	If you knew that the boy who bugs you while you play basketball with your friends has a medical condition that makes him say and do odd things, would you act differently?
If you knew that the girl you think is pretty and smart has a very hard life at home and feels unloved, would you be nicer to her?	If you knew that the boy who sits beside you in class and says funny things can't help saying those things out loud, would you still make fun of him?
If you knew that when you pushed that boy down on the ground he was very embarrassed, would you act differently?	If you knew that when your two friends played together after school they talked about what a nice person you are, would you still be jealous that they had a playdate and did not invite you?
If you knew that when you laughed at your friend because she can't read she went home and yelled at her little sister, would you act differently?	If you knew that when you provoked the boy in your class to get upset and have a meltdown he got suspended from school, would you act differently?
If you knew that the boy you yelled at and told you did not like him has been sad all week, would you be nicer to him?	If you knew that people were a little scared of you when you yell, would you stop yelling?

3. Have them silently consider the questions.
4. To extend the activity, you can make an Action–Consequence chart with students. See sample on page 130. Use the chart to visually demonstrate the first negative Action–Consequence by writing and/or drawing what the student did and how it made another feel. In the lower section, show a positive redo for an Action–Consequence by brainstorming a different action and showing how it would make the child feel.

PROBLEM	ACTION	CONSEQUENCE
Your friend upsets you.	You yell at her and tell her you don't like her.	She goes home feeling very sad.
REDO		
Your friend upsets you.	You ask her to please stop doing what she is doing.	Your friend stops upsetting you and you keep playing.

Discussion Before and After

- Discuss how individual actions can affect how a person feels about themselves.
- Reflect on a time you said something to someone and his/her face turned from happy to sad.

Moment-to-Moment Support

Understanding the Skill Deficit

Some children's intense emotions of jealousy or insecurity lead to behaviors that escalate situations and result in worse outcomes for them and for others. Help children understand that, if they feel jealous of others, then they need to think of a positive first step into play instead of a negative one.

Model

"It is important to take the time to think about the needs and thoughts of others. As your teacher, I have to know you, your strengths as well as your struggles, in order to be able to help you day to day."

Chase the Skill

How you react to a child making fun of another or being judgmental with another will create the climate of your classroom. Try not to ignore a child who has put down another; it sends a message that it is okay to treat a classmate that way. Try not to reprimand a child who has put down another child; it sends the confusing message that a child cannot judge another child, but a teacher can. Address the situation (not the child), either immediately or at the next available opportunity. Examine the issue as a class: "Class, when a friend in our class does something that surprises us or that we think does not make sense, should we react to it and let our friend know that we think it is odd or should we focus on ourselves?" If the child who put down another knows that you are talking about him/her, be sure to approach the child later on in private. Reassure the child that he/she should not feel guilty or ashamed of what happened. Indicate that the focus should not be on what he/she did, but about what he/she will do next time.

6

Actively Developing Cognitive Skills

Attending

Looking Beyond the Behavior

In a student with weak attending skills, you will observe
- student does not pay attention to what others want him/her to
- student does not stay on task and is easily distracted
- student starts a task but does not complete it

Understanding Attending Skills

Some children are able to attend with great focus when they are engaged in an activity that they like and are interested in; however, when it comes to a task they do not enjoy or when it is another person who is speaking or taking a turn, they shut down and stop attending. This results in lack of work completion in school, and in frustration for those who are trying to help the child and for peers who are working with him/her. We want to help children stay focused on a task and continue to engage in it, even when it is not their turn to participate. We want to help children attend while another child is engaged in a task.

Active Skill Development

- to practice paying attention and staying focused on a non-preferred task

The Pathway

Instructions

Grades K–3
Approximate Time: 30 minutes

Instead of paper, you can use mats. Or you can use chalk or tape to mark squares on the floor. You can simplify the game by using a different color for each square.

1. Place 12 large pieces of paper on the floor in four rows of three.
2. Choose a student to be the Mapper. He/she creates a pathway of squares for the other children to guess.
3. The Mapper creates a map by drawing the 12 squares and marking the pathway. Starting with a square in the row closest to him/her and finishing with a square in the row farthest away, the Mapper chooses five squares in between.
4. Have students line up at the closest row.
5. Students take turns being the Guesser. The Guesser steps on a square and looks to the Mapper. Without speaking, the Mapper will indicate if the square

is included in his/her map by nodding. If the square is not on the map, the Mapper shakes his/her head, and the next student becomes the Guesser.

6. Each Guesser continues to guess, one square at a time, until the Mapper indicates the Guesser has guessed a wrong square. Then the next student becomes the Guesser.

7. Working as a team and using the information revealed by the students ahead in line, the students work out the correct pathway.

Discussion Before and After

- Discuss how important it is to concentrate even when it is not your turn.
- Reflect on the strategies students used to remember which squares were on the correct path.

Moment-to-Moment Support

Praise the Learning Process

Remind students ahead of time that they are a team, working together, and that they need to concentrate during another child's turn and use that information. Also, they need to encourage their friends, and not get upset if someone makes a guess that has already been tried. A way of keeping the game fun and non-competitive is to not keep track of how many turns it takes to guess the correct pathway. As well, the person who guesses the last correct square is not the winner of the game. Focus on the fact that the group solved the pathway together.

Understanding the Skill Deficit

When a student is distracted, he/she is not deliberately trying to disobey or frustrate you. He/she most likely has full intentions of following through on the task; however, his/her mind loses focus on it. To support the student, consistently cue him/her nonverbally back to the task by pointing to where he/she should be looking and where his/her body should be. You can add verbal information to remind the student about focusing: "Right now our brains should be focused on one task. We have one job to do and our brains need to be thinking about what steps are involved in that task."

Scaffolding

Be flexible and willing to modify your expectations according to the individual learning style of a student. Observe what the student is doing in order to learn and support his/her learning style. For example, if Jenny learns better by holding a book to her face because she sees the text better and is less distracted, allow her to learn that way.

Sensory Breaks

Use natural breaks in the lesson to recharge students' brains. When the whole class has finished reading and before starting written book work, take a few minutes to get organized. Let the children stretch, get water, or jump up and down.

Nonverbal Cues

Decrease verbal correction and the use of a student's name to cue him/her. Avoid using a child's name multiple times, as this repetition can have a negative social impact. Use nonverbal pointing, cueing, and body movement (e.g., adjust shoulders and head so they are looking where they should).

Homework

Send home a description of the activity. Include these suggestions:

> Playdates can be hard for children who struggle socially. For playdates, it is always important to pick an activity based on the dynamic between your child and the other child. This is an excellent game to play with your child and a similarly challenged peer, offering interaction opportunities and requiring cooperation. If the children butt heads, help them play this game together.

Switching Modalities

Looking Beyond the Behavior

In a student with weak skills of switching modalities, you will observe
- student requires sustained, one-dimensional effort to engage in tasks
- student has a hard time with tasks that require two skills or switching from one skill to another

Understanding the Skill of Switching Modalities

Some children listen to music while they do their homework, while others have a hard time talking or working once the music comes on. For these children, it is difficult to simultaneously process two skills: i.e., the input and output of language, speaking and listening. But it is also hard for them to switch back and forth between the two. It is important to respect this skill deficit in the classroom and to understand that a child might not hear information given in the background while working in a group. Social engagement is all about switching back and forth from listening to speaking and, as groups increase in size, sometimes a child needs to be able to do both at the same time, or he/she misses key decisions the group makes.

Active Skill Development

- to learn to attend to multiple sources of information and alternate between them

Who Is in My Group?

Instructions

Grades 1–6
Approximate Time: 30 minutes

1. Tell students you will be assigning them an animal by whispering to them, by showing a picture of the animal, or by showing the word written down. Assign the same animal to four students.
2. At your signal, students move around the room making the sound of their animal. They are not allowed to speak or make any other noise.

3. As they go around the room, they listen for another making the same sound.
4. When they find another student with the same animal, they pair together and continue to search for others.
5. When they have found their group of four, the group sits down.
6. You can extend this game by having students act out or describe the animals. You can use transportation vehicles, superheroes, etc. instead of animals.

Discussion Before and After

- Discuss how the task required that they make noise to give information, while also listening to get information.
- Reflect on the strategies they used to concentrate on two different things at once.

Moment-to-Moment Support

Zone of Proximal Development

Be sure to pick simple animals for younger children and more difficult animals for older children; i.e., cats and dogs are easy, whereas donkeys and giraffes are harder. In order to support the children who might not do well in this task, make their group bigger. For example, you could have more children who are dogs so that children who struggle can find each other more easily, and there will be more of them to help each other.

Verbal Thinking Cues

Have key words to help cue students during this activity and in the classroom. This concept might be frustrating to you as a teacher, since you feel that all information you give them is important and they should always be attending; however, that is not the reality in the classroom or in life. So when presenting safety information or key learning information, it helps to pause and cue the students to the fact that you are about to say something they should listen to: "I am about to say something very important" or "Listen to this."

Nonverbal Cues

Point to your ears to show students that it takes effort to listen and attend.

Self-Talk

"I was so focused on making my animal sound that I was not thinking about listening. It is important to think about listening too. I will not find my teammates if I focus my brain only on making my animal sound."

Information Sequencing

Looking Beyond the Behavior

In a student with weak information sequencing skills, you will observe
- student does not accurately visually process information
- student does not attend visually or look around to observe the environment

Understanding Information Sequencing Skills

We want to help children focus their concentration on a sequential task, put it into memory, and be able to recall it. Children with visual processing challenges are able to see, but they might not look around the environment and attend to visual information, or might be unable to appropriately store and use the information they see to perform a task or access information. In class, we typically accommodate non-visual learners with auditory instructions; we use language to describe what their brains are not processing visually. This is a great teaching strategy to support the student, but we should never give up on building the skill by helping him/her attend to visual stimuli and practice storing the information.

Active Skill Development

- to develop the ability to look to, attend, and process information in a sequence

Line Them Up

Instructions

Grades 1–6
Approximate Time: 15 minutes

1. Have a number of students come to the front of the class. Base the number on the recall ability of your students: for how peers many will students be able to remember the order?
2. Have students stand in a straight line, facing the class.
3. Allow students at their desks 10 seconds, or sufficient time to focus and process the information, to remember the students and the order they are standing in.
4. Have students in line return to their desks.
5. Ask for two volunteers from the rest of the class to work together to call the students who had been in line to the front of the room and line them up again.

Discussion Before and After

- Discuss what memory tricks and tools students use to remember the order.
- Reflect on a school task that requires these same skills.

Moment-to-Moment Support

Structure

Teachers are often expected to visually and auditorily chunk information for students; this is an opportunity to teach students how to chunk on their own. For this activity, have each student in line hold up a large piece of paper with his/her name on it and his/her number in the line order. Have students visually take in the students and the numbers. Then, as a class, chant the sequence to help students remember the sequence. You can vary this activity by having half the class call the number and the other half call out the child's name.

Chase the Skill

Once you have done this activity a few times and the children understand sequencing, use nonverbal social interactions within the class as a way of communicating who is the next in line. Tell students they need to determine who they think was the next in line, but they need to yell out the person's name as a group consensus, all at once. With no talking ahead of calling out the name, students will need to look at each other and point, nodding and shaking their heads to come to a consensus. Once they all agree, they can signal to each other that they want to call out the name.

Nonverbal Cues

Point to where the child should look instead of telling the child to pay attention.

Peer Facilitation

Have students who are easily able to perform this task explain to the class what method they use to chunk the information.

Seeing the Whole Picture

Looking Beyond the Behavior

In students with weak skills of seeing the whole picture, you will observe
- student will notice little details, but will miss attending to the lesson, the game, or what another is saying
- student misses the underlying point, idea, or concepts

Understanding the Skills of Seeing the Whole Picture

Some children focus on detail in the environment. This is a great skill to have, as it allows them to notice and observe key elements; it often underlies a talent like the ability to draw in detail and create intricate maps. However, having an intense focus on details sometimes means that they miss the whole picture and the intended message. In class, sometimes a student is so busy concentrating on one aspect of the assignment that he/she is unable to put the assignment together as a whole.

Active Skill Development

- to be able to focus on one task while maintaining an awareness of the environment as a whole

What Is Going On in the Background

Instructions

Grades K–3
Approximate Time: 30 minutes

1. Have students sit in a circle, or arrange desks to form a large circle with a space in the middle.

2. Have three students be on the red team, wearing red. Have another three students on a team of another color. Have both teams pass a ball around the centre of the circle.
3. Ask students to count how many times members of the red team pass the ball to each other.
4. Explain that you will do three things while the students pass the ball, and that they will be asked what you did. With younger students, use big, obvious actions; e.g., jumping jacks or pushups. With older students, the actions can be more subtle; e.g., hold up four fingers or tap your head.

Discussion Before and After

- Discuss how students had to move their eyes back and forth to complete two tasks at the same time.
- Reflect on the strategies they used to continue counting while trying to notice and remember your actions.

Moment-to-Moment Support

Zone of Proximal Development

In order to ensure success, be sure to make this activity appropriate for the age and skill levels of your students. You might begin by doing one very obvious thing; for example, you might go into the middle of the circle and do one jumping jack. As students get used to attending to two things and going back and forth with their eyes, make your movements more subtle; for example, you might scratch your nose.

Verbal Thinking Cue

"This task requires two focuses. We need to focus hard and concentrate on tracking the ball and the red team, but we can't over-focus on the detail. We need to look at the big picture and examine the important background information. We need to shift our focus inward and outward from the big picture to the detail and back. This skill is required often in life. We need to focus on our friends, but we need to look out and observe the whole situation."

Praise the Learning Process

If you do work with a child who often gets caught up in small details, catch him/her when he/she is caught up in the whole process. For example, "I think the reason you are enjoying this game is that you are not stopping to focus on the little issues. Your eyes are not focusing on one detail; they are scanning the game and the activity itself. I think that is why you are having fun with it and enjoying yourself."

Regulate the Environment

Some children get caught up in and distracted by peripheral noises or visuals. When you can, allow the child time to go into a room, examine it, walk around, and ask a few questions before you want the child's attention. Once you begin the task, he/she will have already had a chance to look at and say what he/she needed to and might be more able to focus on the activity.

Flexibility

Looking Beyond the Behavior

In a student with weak flexibility skills, you will observe
- student gets stuck on one idea or outcome
- student tries the same solution or expresses the same thought repeatedly, even if it does not work and is not accepted by others
- student struggles with shifting his/her thinking and with attempting a new strategy

Understanding Flexibility Skills

Hide and Seek is a hard game for children to learn. They usually hide and look in the same spot over and over again. It gets easier as they learn to be more creative in their ideas and more open to new possibilities. But for some children, this is a long learning process and it affects many areas of their lives. We need to demonstrate to children the importance of looking at other options and solutions when the most logical answer is not available. In class, we expect children to be accommodating of, adaptable to, and flexible with the needs and wants of others; when a child is not, we assume it is within the child's control and he/she is choosing to be difficult. It is important to see flexibility of movement and thought as a skill that comes easily to some but not to others, as opposed to as a character quality that makes a child bad, difficult, or controlling.

Active Skill Development

- to be able to adapt and alter what one thinks, needs, and wants in response to the needs of others

Indoor Hide and Seek

Instructions

Grades K–3
Approximate Time: 30 minutes

1. Have students sitting comfortably. Present an object to the class.
2. Choose one student to be the Hider.
3. While the other students keep their eyes closed, the Hider places the object in view somewhere in the classroom.
4. Once the Hider sits down, the other students open their eyes and look for the object. They remain seated at their desks, and cannot ask questions.
5. If the students cannot find the object, the Hider can give clues.
6. Once the students have found the object, another Hider is chosen and the game is repeated.

To ensure success, start off having a large object hidden in a small room.

Discussion Before and After

- Discuss the impact of not thinking of new and creative places to put an object, but just copying what the previous Hider did.
- Reflect on a time a child could not think of something new and did the same thing over and over again.

Moment-to-Moment Support

Structure

Show children different levels and heights in the room. Most classroom materials should be placed low for the children and should be easily accessible. Take advantage of games like this to push the boundaries of the room and to have children look up high and under objects in an exploration of the room.

Verbal Thinking Cue

"In order to shift our mindset, we need to practice being flexible in our thoughts and ideas. We need to look with our eyes around the environment and try different options and alternatives. If we stay focused on one solution, we limit our possibilities."

Scaffolding

A child who is rigid will struggle on the carpet or in a group situation. His/her play will not switch easily to follow the play of others; he/she will have difficulty following objects, movement, and ideas. Supporting this child cannot be done verbally at a distance. For example, it will not help if you tell the student to share or be flexible, or if you instruct him/her to respect others' choices. These command statements will only place demands on the child and increase his/her level of stress, therefore increasing his/her rigidity. Helping this child must come through proximal support: sitting with the child and facilitating the play. Try to support the ideas of the other children; for example, if another child suggests a strategy, nod your head and indicate that you think that idea is great. Verbally praise and reinforce the play of other children, making another child's ideas and strategies seem interesting and neat: "Cool, what a great idea. I would never have thought about doing our project that way, but that sounds fantastic."

Peer Scaffolding

- Have a student's peers help explain their thoughts and needs to a child who is rigid instead of directing the problem-solving yourself. For example, Marsha is controlling what the other students can and can't do, do not tell Marsha to let the others play the way they want, and do not tell the other student to ignore Marsha. Help the other students explain to Marsha that they also get to have ideas and to play the way they want.
- If you closely examine the dynamics between a cognitively inflexible student and his/her peers, you might see the peers beginning to accept the inflexible one as the authority and to ask for permission from him/her. It is important to help children understand that if they keep asking permission of the inflexible student, they are giving a lot of power to him/her. Support the other students in exerting their own rights and choices: e.g., help them say, "I will be the narrator" instead of, "Marsha, can I be the narrator?"

Symbolic Thinking

Looking Beyond the Behavior

In a student with weak symbolic thinking skills, you will observe
- student is literal in his/her interpretations of the world and language
- student does not engage in creative and imaginary play

Understanding Symbolic Thinking Skills

Help children increase their thinking flexibility by demonstrating that there is not just one answer or one function for an object. Socially, children can struggle during play as they become set in specific ways to play with objects and specific functions for things. Successful creative and imaginary play necessitates the ability to see beyond the intended purpose or function of objects and people, and to be flexible in language and ideas. For some children, this is very difficult. We can help these children be less rigid in their understanding and to allow them to explore different uses for the toys and objects in their class.

Active Skill Development

- to be able to think of things in abstract, varied, and non-literal ways

What Is It?

Instructions

Grades 1–6
Approximate Time: 30 minutes

1. Have students sit in a circle.
2. From a box full of regular classroom objects (e.g., pencil, book, ball, CD), pick one object and place it in the middle of the circle.
3. When they are ready, students put up their hands for a turn.
4. One student at a time comes up and takes the object. Without words, the student pretends the object is something else and acts out the use of the imagined object. For example, a pencil can be a microphone, telephone, drumstick; a CD can be a steering wheel or a dish.
5. Once all students are comfortable with and successful at this activity, they can pass the object around the circle to show the imagined use of it.

Discussion Before and After

- Discuss the benefit of being creative with things and open to new ideas.
- Reflect on whether a student had a hard time thinking of the object in different ways.

Moment-to-Moment Support

Grouping

This is an excellent activity to do with age-based heterogenous grouping. It takes a bit of organization, but is an effective teaching technique. If you scaffold heterogenous groups so that a strong student helps a peer through an activity, certain children will begin to take on a role of being supported, without ever playing the role of supporter. If a student in the class is rarely stronger than his/her peers at any skill, then this child needs to support younger children. Coordinate with teachers in your school to create heterogenous groups made up of an older student who struggles at the skill and younger children the older student can learn with and teach.

Sarcasm is an important form of social interaction that you should help students identify. Teach the difference between friendly sarcasm, which is meant as a form of joking and does not poke fun at another person, and mean sarcasm, which is specifically designed to make fun of another person.

Verbal Thinking Cue

"We need to keep in mind how we were able to be flexible with our play during this game. Sometimes when we play with our friends, we become fixed in our way of thinking and want the play to go a certain way. If we remember how much fun we had today being creative and flexible, we can try to allow our friends to bring their ideas into our play."

Chase the Skill

Some children who take things literally do not understand sarcasm. This is why it is always recommended that teachers not use sarcasm with students, especially with those who do not get it. This is true to a point: never use sarcasm to make fun of a child or to be mean to a child; do not use sarcasm in discipline. Considering the stress levels described in Teach/Practice/Survive on page 28, never use sarcasm with a child when the child is in a state of high stress, the survival stage. But you can carefully use friendly sarcasm with a child in a state of medium stress, the practice stage. This will support the child in understanding sarcasm during social interactions. Finally, you can consistently use friendly sarcasm when a child is in a state of low stress, the teaching stage.

Homework

Send home a description of the activity. Include these suggestions:

> Teach your child idioms as a way of showing the difference between literal and figurative speaking. Some idioms:
> - Break a leg.
> - Stay the course.
> - Let the dust settle.
> - Don't trust someone as far as you can throw them.
> - Quick on the draw.

Recognizing Character

Looking Beyond the Behavior

In a student with weak skills of understanding character, you will observe
- student describes and identifies others with a single physical or action description, instead of what they are like as people

Understanding the Skill of Recognizing Character

Many children have difficulty understanding the perspectives of others because they have varying abilities to see others as people with personalities, thoughts, intentions, and motives. Children need to identify others in multiple ways, including using personal character qualities, temperament, and interests. Children who are successful in social play look at their friends and see more than the physical features; they view others as the whole of their parts. When thinking about each friend, they recall information about the person's personality, preferences, and experiences. We need to teach some children to think about others in more social detail.

Active Skill Development

- to increase understanding of the attributes that make up a person's character

Character Profiles

Instructions

Grades K–6
Approximate Time: 30 minutes

You can help strengthen students' executive function by creating a time delay between the student hearing the direction and having to perform the task. Wait five seconds after telling them the character before signaling students to start acting.

1. Have students spread out around the room.
2. Give students a character to act out; choose from the list below or come up with your own.
3. Students must not use words, but need to think about what actions, body language, and gestures to use to portray the character. Students can close their eyes if it makes them more comfortable.
4. Write the character on the board and discuss what students did to act out the character: e.g., for Police Officer, they acted out confidence, strength; they stood up straight and put hands on belt; they wrote a ticket or helped someone.
5. Together, create a character profile for the character.

SAMPLE CHARACTERS

Prince/Princess	Teacher	Chef	Fire Fighter
Circus Performer	Babysitter	Mom	Runner
Old Man	Police Officer	Knight	Batman
Rescue Hero	Cat	Cheerleader	Dog
Artist	Waiter	Doctor	Magician
Baby	Store Owner	Hair Dresser	Dad
Ballet Dancer	Horse	Flamingo	King/Queen

Discussion Before and After

- Discuss how students knew what to do to act out the character.
- Reflect on what they did and thought about in order to act as the character.

Moment-to-Moment Support

Verbal Thinking Cue

"Great work, Tina. I can see the strong personality of your librarian in the expression on your face."

Grouping

Use a round-robin technique for this activity. This technique involves homogenous grouping and heterogenous grouping for the same activity and is an excellent way to simultaneously provide a child with initial exposure to an activity at his/her level and also exposure to the activity just beyond his/her ability with support from his/her peer group. First, place the class in homogenous groups and allow them time to do the activity together at their ability level. Then, switch groups so that each new group is comprised of members from each of the old groups.

Social Cognition

Looking Beyond the Behavior

In a student with weak social cognition skills, you will observe
- student is unaware of him/herself and his/her own character qualities
- student is unaware of the impact of his/her character on others

Understanding Social Cognition Skills

If we want children to be able to self-monitor, it is important that we show them the qualities that contribute positively to friendship, group discussions, and play. Group work is a challenging part of school for some children. The dynamics of different children can result in arguments and negative experiences. When creating groups for any activity or project, it is important to look at which children can work well together and place them accordingly. It is also important to help children understand the different qualities they can bring to the group in a supportive and productive way.

Active Skill Development

- to build self-awareness and awareness of others as it applies to social situations and qualities

Positive Influencer

Instructions

Grades 1–6
Approximate Time: 30 minutes

1. Start with the whole class. Have students sit at their desks or in a large circle.
2. Tell students you will be working as a class to examine different qualities that help support group work and influence a group in a positive way.
3. Choose a character from the list below. Students imitate the words, body language, tone, and/or facial expressions of the quality the character embodies.
4. Pick student volunteers to act in front of the class, one at a time.
5. Expand into role-play scenarios of situations similar to the struggles students face in the classroom. Choose two students to act together in front of the class. Have them play the same positive quality; e.g., Mrs. Yes and Mr. Yes. Then have the students play different positive qualities.
6. Create a chart of the actions that made students successful in acting out the quality.

SAMPLE CHARACTERS BASED ON QUALITIES

Ms. Yes	Ms. Sure-That-Sounds-Good	Mr. Okay-I-agree
Mr. Encourager		Sir That-Is-A-Great-Idea
Ms. Lighthearted	Dr. Think Positively	Count Flexible
Miss Organizer	Mr. Energizer	Mrs. Nice
Mrs. I-Love-Everything	Mr. Peacekeeper	Professor Friendly
Sir Forgiving	Sir Helper	Mrs. Good Listener

Miss I-Will-Focus-On-Myself	Mr. Speak-In-A-Soft-Tone	Dr. Everyone-Can-Learn-From-Their-Mistakes
Ms. Everyone-Should-Have-a-Turn	Ms. Let-Me-Explain-It–One-More-Time	
Ms. I-Can-Nod-In-Agreement-While-You-Talk	Dr. You-Have-the-Right-to-Your-Ideas	

Discussion Before and After

- Discuss the effect of a strong personality and how it can take over and affect how other people feel.
- Reflect on how a student felt when another student acted out a negative personality or a positive one.

Moment-to-Moment Support

Model

The most important way to help children is to show them what they should do to be successful. If you have a student who is always negative and disagrees with everything, be sure to consistently have him/her act out Mr. Yes, Mr. Sure-That-Sounds-Good, Mr. Okay-I-Agree. Show that student the positive impact these qualities will have on friends.

Grouping

Consider your students' character qualities when grouping. What is easier is not always the best learning opportunity, so consider the level of stress of the activity in determining the way you will pair children. If the activity is a high-stress activity (difficult, dynamic, unstructured, or using imagination), pair a rigid thinker with a flexible thinker. Any conflict will likely come because the flexible child will appease the needs of the less flexible one. When the activity is less stressful (highly motivated, structured, with clear rules), consider pairing a rigid student with a student who will push back and self-assert.

Chase the Skill

Do not focus on the skill development of only the students whose negative behavior catches your attention. Chase the skill development of all students in the class. The appeaser in your class is often helped the least. It is a wonderful quality to consistently mitigate situations, to be flexible to the needs of others, and to seek to please other children and the teacher. However, it can lead to a child who is not self-advocating and does not take any social risks to please him/herself. Over time, children who consistently feel that they have to give in to the needs of others to help mitigate a negative situation can become resentful. Be sure to support these children too, even if it means you create a conflict in the facilitation where there wasn't one. For example, if you are in a state of low stress and have time to facilitate a discussion between Marsha and a peer who is appeasing her every need, come into the discussion and help the other child have a stronger voice.

Role-play can be daunting for anyone. Children are unpredictable and the lack of structure makes role-play a little scary to take on. But do take it on. Role-play is the most effective way for children to practice and understand challenging social nuances. Be proactive and set it up for success. Plan your space; let students know exactly where to sit and how to sit; detail your expectations, for example, "While role-playing, we do not touch our friends. We keep our hands to ourselves."

Behavior Modulation

Looking Beyond the Behavior

In a student with weak behavior modulation skills, you will observe
- student does not understand exactly how to behave in social situations
- students does not understand which behaviors lead to positive social success and which behaviors lead to negative social interactions

Understanding Behavior Modulation Skills

Social behavior is complex and dynamic, and requires many adjustments in thinking through interactions. Some children need detailed instruction and visual support for exactly what they should say and do during different social dynamics. It is not enough to tell some children to stop talking so much or to listen more closely. It is not helpful to say, "You need to work on your conversation skills." Some children need explicit help breaking down social expectations of conversations and then they need to be supported to practice these skills.

Active Skill Development

- to understand which behaviors will lead to social success and to alter and adjust behaviors to be socially successful

Visual Action Plan

Instructions

Grades K–6
Approximate Time: 30–45 minutes.

1. Create a two-column chart on the board. Head one column *Negative Impact*, and the other *Positive Impact*.
2. Choose an event or situation to review with the class; e.g., an upcoming field trip. Start writing and/or drawing all behaviors connected with the event that would result in negative consequences. For example, *running on the road, not staying with the group, talking loudly on the bus, being rude to the tour guide.* Explain how these actions would make you feel: "These actions would worry me as a teacher. I might not feel safe taking the class on another field trip." Go into specific detail in a neutral tone, not mockingly, punitively, or meanly.
3. Act out the behaviors, allowing the class to laugh together and have fun.

4. For each Negative Impact behavior, write and draw in detail a corresponding Positive Impact behavior. Include details of what the student would be doing and thinking.
5. Ask students how they think positive or negative behavior will affect others. For example, "How do you think that would make me feel on the field trip? How would that behavior make your friend feel?"
6. Act out each behavior. Be sure to exaggerate your positive response to Positive Impact behaviors.

Discussion Before and After

- Discuss how other people feel in reaction to your behavior.
- Reflect on a time when your behavior had a positive impact on the outcome of an activity or task.

Moment-to-Moment Support

Proactive Support

If a student consistently struggles with a particular event, offer choices of behavior to the student before the event itself. Offer one choice that resembles the negative behavior usually exhibited and offer another choice detailing positive behavior the child could show instead. For example, before Marsha works on a project with a peer, you say to her, "Will this project go well and will your partner be happy if you decide the topic, pick each section, and tell her what to do? Or will your partner be happy if she gets a say in the topic and if you listen to her thoughts and ideas?" Consider giving the student one first strategy or sentence to begin with; for example, "Marsha, you could start by asking your partner what she would be interested in studying."

Model

Let students know that you also need help checking which behaviors you should and should not use. Let them watch you plan in explicit detail what you will try to do as a teacher and what you will try not to do. Make the chart with them. Let them see you as a person who is trying each day to do the best job you can.

Detailed Positive Praise

Always use praise that is focused on the behavior, not the character. For example, use how Billy is behaving to describe to Todd how he should be sitting and why he should sit that way: "Todd look at how Billy is sitting. His bum is on the chair, his legs hang down to the ground, and his hands are on the desk. His body is facing forward and his eyes are on the teacher. This way, he is not distracted and his eyes and ears will be paying attention and help him follow the lesson."

Remember, never call attention to behavior to compare the character of two students. Help students learn from each other in a positive non-competitive way that objectively compares actions, but does not judge character or compare the students as people.

Social Narration

Looking Beyond the Behavior

In a student with weak social narration skills, you will observe
- student is unable to explain or share social events of the day
- student does not transfer information from one setting to another

Understanding Social Narration Skills

Some children have a hard time retelling what happens at school. Instead of sending a note home to the parent that describes what a child did or what happened to the child, you can help make the child part of the process. Use a communication journal, drawn or written from the child's point of view, to communicate with parents.

Active Skill Development

- to learn to explain and retell social events

This Is What Happened

Instructions

Grades 1–6
Approximate Time: 15 minutes

1. A daily journal activity will help students recap what happened, review their thoughts and feelings, and inform their parents about their day. Use the same book students record their homework in, with half the page to note the next day's homework and the other half to reflect on the day.
2. After the occurrence of an event that should be communicated to parents, such as a conflict, have the student draw a picture to indicate what happened. Be sure the picture includes a stick figure, a heart, and a speech balloon.
3. Help the student add accurate detail and words. Suggest the student add a thought bubble and/or a rectangle to describe action. See sample below.
4. Ask the student to take the picture home and explain it to his/her parents.

Throughout this book, shapes are used to show emotions and actions:

♡ Heart = what we feel

▭ Rectangle = what we do

💬 Speech balloon = what we say

💭 Thought bubble = what we think

Discussion Before and After

- Discuss how the pictures helped the student tell the story.
- Reflect on what it is about the drawings that makes it easier for the student to organize his/her thoughts.

Moment-to-Moment Support

Scaffolding

Communicate through, not around, the child. Use this communication journal format to help the student be the communication link between home and school.

SAMPLE *THIS IS WHAT HAPPENED* PAGE

148

7

Dealing with Meltdowns

As we build a child's emotional regulation skills, we can help de-escalate a child's moment-to-moment emotional challenges. When a meltdown is imminent, children benefit from calming down before being directed to problem-solve. So one of the most effective things you can do in a crisis situation is to take a breath, slow yourself down, and approach the situation calmly. Your first priority is to regulate the student.

When a child begins to get upset, rigid, and/or noncompliant, stop trying to solve the problem. First help the child calm down.

This chapter breaks down the stages of a meltdown and identifies how to respond in order to support the student, based on the stage of the student's dysregulation.

Step 1: Stop Talking

Pause during a crisis; try not to teach, discipline, or correct.

Often, an adult's first response to a child beginning to get upset is to try to solve the problem. We continue to teach a skill, we correct and discipline the child, we ask him/her to explain the problem to us, and we try to reason with him/her. As children continue to fail to do what we want or think the way we want, we tend to jump in—verbally and nonverbally—to tell, solve, direct, continue to try to teach. This is often when the adult begins to get upset and dysregulate as well. As the adult's stress and inflexibility increase in a situation, so do the child's. This escalates the situation. Adults can unintentionally escalate a situation by

- continuing to explain, teach, and control the activity
- physically moving in quickly
- rushing to fix the problem
- asking the child to explain the problem and say what is wrong
- chasing each argument the child throws out
- overtalking and rationalizing
- judging the child's characteristics or generalizing the problem
- unwittingly using a harsh tone and negative body language

The best reaction you can have to a child beginning to get upset is to stop and think. If we understand what is at the root of the child's behavior, the child's emotional dysregulation, and our own dysregulation, we can better manage and handle challenging moments with the child. Before teaching the child self-regulation, consider reflecting on your own.

Step 2: Stop Your Own Escalation

If we start to monitor our own behavior as much as we monitor the child's, it can help de-escalate situations. Once a child emotionally escalates, the adult staying calm, waiting before acting, and giving space are more effective than any suggestion or instruction. Do not misinterpret this message—it does not mean adults cause emotional escalation or that, if the adult simply stays calm, the child will not escalate. But consider slowing down your own actions, determining your strategy, and then proceeding with caution! As the child becomes upset, consider

- not talking.
- not explaining, teaching, telling the child why he/she needs to do something or understand something
- not moving your body toward the child
- listening first
- not getting sidetracked by each argument and objection
- not bringing in past arguments or behavior
- monitoring your own negative body language
- not trying to fix the problem, but instead focusing on calming down the child

Step 3: Stop the Child's Escalation

The first step in stopping a challenging situation from escalating to a meltdown is calming down the child. We have to teach children to calm down separately from trying to reason with them and solve the problem. If a child begins to get upset, we rush to the child and ask him/her what the problem is. Sometimes this action gets the child even more upset. We then try to help the child explain the problem and talk about it. Once the child has explained, we try to help the child understand that it is not such a big problem, or that he/she misunderstood, or that there is an easy solution. At this point we begin to engage in a back-and-forth to try to help the child rethink the problem.

Sometimes this leads to an explosion or a meltdown. What did we miss?

We missed that the child is emotionally overwhelmed by something and we are trying to help the child cognitively instead of emotionally. The child's attention is focused narrowly on the issue at hand. He/she is flooded with emotion and cannot use reason. We need to help the child through his/her senses, not through language. We have to help the child use his/her self-regulation strategies to relax his/her body physically.

Regulating the Dysregulation

- Support the student through the emotional dysregulation by helping him/her breathe to calm down, look out the window to help his/her brain get unstuck, etc.
- Find a spot for the student to go to where he/she will no longer be triggered by what is upsetting him/her. Over time and with practice, the student will be motivated to remove him/herself because he/she understands that it helps him/her calm down.
- Do not tell the student why he/she is wrong or has misinterpreted the problem.
- Do not punish, reprimand, or problem-solve. Instead, help the student learn to calm him/herself.

- Use one consistent method of self-regulation to help one student or the whole class calm down. Use a cue to signal to use the technique. For example, as a class you could decide that, whenever anyone is upset, he/she close his/her eyes and imagine that he/she is blowing up ten balloons as slowly as possible.

A meltdown continues to escalate as long as the child does not get what he/she wants. In some cases, we have to see through the meltdown because we simply cannot accommodate what the child wants and give in to the him/her. In these cases we should not negotiate and should simply support the dysregulation. For example, if Marsha is getting upset that she can't go first for every activity every day, it is important to set rules and schedules that allow all students a turn. Marsha would need to be told that she cannot go first if it is someone else's turn, even if she has a meltdown. But once the meltdown begins, the teacher should follow the steps to support Marsha and not focus on explaining to Marsha the rules of fairness and turn-taking.

In some cases, the issue the child is getting upset about is something we could simply change our mind about and allow him/her to get what he/she wants. But we do not want to give into a child *because* the child is upset. If a child begins to get upset and we provide him/her with what he/she wants in order to stop the negative behavior, we reinforce that negative behavior. For example, if a child starts yelling at peers for behavior that displeases him/her, we should not then tell the others to stop the behavior just to keep the dysregulated child from escalating and getting more upset. That child should not directly associate his/her dysregulation with getting what he/she wants. If you can help the child regulate first, then you can support him/her in self-advocacy, so that he/she associates getting what he/she wants with calm self-advocacy instead of with dysregulation.

Marsha

Outside on the playground, Marsha begins to get upset because the other students are pulling leaves off the trees. The teacher's first instinct is to tell Marsha that it is okay for the other students to pull leaves off trees; that it is not a big deal. Once into this interaction, the teacher quickly realizes that Marsha is extremely upset and is going to have a full meltdown. The teacher also realizes that there is not enough time to support Marsha through a crisis. It would not be helpful to Marsha in the long run for the teacher to quickly give in to her because she is upset. It would not be productive for the teacher to say, "Okay, everyone, stop pulling leaves off the trees, because it really upsets Marsha." This statement tells Marsha that her negative behavior gets her what she wants. However, it would be helpful to Marsha if the teacher was able to calm her down enough to help her ask the other students to stop, and to associate her success in getting what she wants with her calm behavior: "Marsha, I can't come over to help you when you are yelling at your friends and being unkind to them. But I know your friends well and we are a group that listens to each other and accommodates each other. I can help you talk with your friends once we have calmed down. Maybe we should start with five slow breaths before we talk with our friends." In this situation, Marsha will get what she wants, but she gets it by calmly talking with her friends and explaining her point of view. This is a skill that will help Marsha throughout her life.

Preventing Meltdowns

We want to be able to support the child in calming down and continuing to engage in the activity that was interrupted by the meltdown. But some children do not have these skills. If we understand a child's ability to regulate as a skill separate from the activity or task the class is engaged in, it will help us recognize the point at which the only support that we provide the child should be moment-to-moment support for self-regulation.

> Recall the Teach/Practice/Survive process from Chapter 1. Teaching and practicing occur in low- and medium-stress situations, the usual classroom environment:
> - Teach and Practice = Moment-to-moment support of the skill, activity, or task that you were engaged in
>
> Once the situation triggers a high-stress reaction, we must to survival mode:
> - Survive = Moment-to-moment support of child's self-regulation

As the child learns emotional regulation tools, we can help de-escalate the moment-to-moment emotional challenges by
- walking over calmly and slowing down the situation
- showing warmth and empathy in your response
- trying to calm the child before talking or listening to him/her
- having the child sit or go to somewhere removed from the trigger situation
- asking the child to sit down and take ten deep breaths
- using as little language as possible to begin with; showing exaggerated non-verbal support (e.g., showing empathy and calm in face and body)
- listening to the child, his/her concerns, his/her interpretation and view of the event; empathizing with and reflecting on it
- gently and calmly explaining other possible interpretations and perspectives of the event that triggered the upset
- whenever possible, seeing the child through the emotional dysregulation by staying to support and guide him/her through the strong emotions
- behaving without fear, giving the message that both adult and child should not fear outbursts

Actively Developing De-Escalation

Looking Beyond the Behavior

In a student prone to escalation into meltdown, you will observe
- student gets very upset, engages in behavior that makes the problem worse
- student is not able to stay calm and work through a problem in a positive way

Understanding De-Escalation Skills

Children need to recognize the moment their own action becomes a problem. They need to understand and make choices to make a problem go away. They can learn how to stop a problem only if they understand that their social success depends on their own action plan, not on the actions of anyone else.

As long as you try to teach two skills at once, you will escalate the challenging behavior. As child begins to calm down, if we keep focusing on problem-solving the issue and telling the child what he/she is doing wrong, the child will begin to get upset again. As the child calms down, we tell him/her what he/she is doing wrong and start telling him/her what he/she needs to do. Then the child gets upset again.

Active Skill Development

- to understand how little problems turn into big problems
- to examine when, where, and how actions influence the outcome
- to redo a situation and act differently.

Predictable Escalation Skit

Instructions

Grades 1–6
Approximate Time: 30 minutes

1. Together, create and look at a skit that shows the escalation of a problem; see sample on page 154. Read over the whole skit, from little problem to big problem.
2. Discuss how a little problem turned into a big problem.
3. Examine where each child's action created a bigger problem. Trace how each action led to a more serious situation.
4. Go back to the first problem and examine thoughts, feelings, and words to come up with a better action choice.

Discussion Before and After

During drama activities, there should be a strict no-touching rule. Students must move in their own space.

- Discuss how negative feelings can lead to actions that cause social problems.
- Reflect on how each action made by one person can lead the other person to make an even worse action.

Moment-to-Moment Support

Peer Facilitation

When intervening while an argument is taking place between two students, do not come in too quickly and do not take over. Come in to support, but do not separate the children and do not set yourself up as the problem-solver. Let them continue to negotiate and solve their issue. Don't be afraid to let it get a little messy—not physically messy—but allow them to speak their minds and express themselves, and ideally come up with a solution.

Detailed Positive Praise

"Great work, Leslie. You stopped a problem. You made great effort. You worked hard to stop a problem from getting worse. You stopped worrying about what the other person did and you focused on your action plan. Well done."

Conclusion

It is only by understanding that all children are unique and capable in their own way that we are able to help them gain an understanding of the social norms and expectations society has of them. This is because, instead of telling, giving direction, and expecting social skills from a child, we must convince children of the social benefits of following society's expectations. As we slowly try to teach a child how to be more social, we begin by better accepting the child for his/her strengths and challenges, and then go on to slowly, deliberately, and positively explain to the child how these skills help him/her learn, make friends, and better succeed.

This process can begin only when we understand the role that we, as educators and parents, play in each interaction. As more people help guide children with empathy and feedback, instead of punishment and direction, they will better understand social nuances and be more motivated to engage and join in.

If I look back at my years as a classroom teacher working with children with Asperger's or ADHD, I recognize my empathy and compassion for them, but I lament my lack of knowledge of how to help them. I knew they experienced challenges in particular areas and I thought that my expectations for these children needed to be different from those I had for their peers. Now I understand that it is not about the expectations being different. It is how we achieve those expectations that is different: for some children it needs to be more deliberate, slower, and with more guidance. Instead of accepting that a child cannot or will not perform a task, and therefore the task itself should be modified, we need to understand that the task is difficult for that child and the process for him/her to get to the task may be different. Do not get angry or frustrated that the child is not succeeding. Change and accommodate the process in order to help the child succeed. And never stop teaching, guiding, prompting, reinforcing, and encouraging the child to perform the task.

Professional Resources

Andrews, Amy (2013) "Teachers unprepared to deal with mental health issues among students" Paper presented at Congress 2013, Federation for the Humanities and Social Sciences; see media release at http://www.congress2013.ca/sites/default/files/sites/default/uploads/congress/Congress2013/media-release-june-1-mh-en.pdf

Bissell, Julie, Jean Fisher, Carol Owens, and Patricia Polcyn (1998) *Sensory Motor Handbook: A Guide for Implementing and Modifying Activities in the Classroom.* Torrance, CA: Sensory Integration International Publishers.

Briers, Stephen (2009) *Brilliant Cognitive Behavioural Therapy.* Toronto, ON: Pearson Prentice Hall.

Burton, Bonnie (2009) *Girls against Girls.* San Francisco, CA: Zest Books.

Clark, Lynn (2005) *SOS for Parents.* Bowling Green, KY: SOS Programs & Parents Press.

Crooke, Pamela and Michelle Garcia Winner (2011) *Social Fortune or Social Fate.* San Jose, CA: Social Thinking Publishing.

Davy, Till (2011) *Developmental Executive Skills Disorder (DESD)* at http://pediatriciantoronto.ca/Dr._Till_Davy_M.D./DESD_-_Developmental_Executive_Skills_Disorder_files/DESD.pdf

Delsandro, M. Elizabeth (2010) *We Can Make It Better.* San Jose, CA: Think Social Publications.

Doherty, Gillian (1998) "Assessing Quality in Child Care Settings" *Interaction*, vol. 12, no. 1, Spring. Canadian Child Care Federation.

Gibbs, Jeanne (2001) *Tribes.* Windsor, CA: Center Source Systems.

Greenberger, Dennis and Christine Padesky (1995) *Mind Over Mood.* New York, NY: Guilford Press.

Greene, Ross (2005) *The Explosive Child.* New York, NY: HarperCollins.

Heegaard, Marge Eaton (2001) *Drawing Together to Learn about Feelings.* Minneapolis, MN: Fairview Press.

Madrigal, Stephanie and Michelle Garcia Winner (2008) *Superflex®: A Superhero Social Thinking Curriculum Package.* San Jose, CA: Social Thinking Publishing.

Pepler, Debra (2006) "Bullying Interventions: A Binocular Perspective" *Canadian Academy of Child & Adolescent Psychiatry*, 15(1): 16–20 at http://www.ncbi.nlm.nih.gov/pmc/articles/PMC2277273/

Pyle, Cary (2009) *Indoor & Outdoor Games.* Westminster, CA: Teacher Created Resources.

Rogers, Sally J. and Geraldine Dawson (2010) *Early Start Denver Model for Young Children with Autism: Promoting Language, Learning, and Engagement.* New York, NY: Guilford Press.

Stock Kranowitz, Carol (2010) *The Out-of-sync Child: Simple and Fun.* New York, NY: Perigee.

Shanker, Stuart (2013) *Calm, Alert, and Learning: Classroom Strategies for Self-Regulation.* Toronto, ON: Pearson.

Sussman, Fern (2006) *TalkAbility.* Toronto, ON: The Hanen Centre.

Swartz, Larry (2002) *The New Dramathemes.* Markham, ON: Pembroke.

VanFleet Risë, Andrea E. Sywulak, and Cynthia Caparosa Sniscak (2010) *Child-Centered Play Therapy.* New York, NY: Guilford Press.

Vgotsky, Lev S. (1986) *Thought and Language* Revised Edition. Cambridge, MA: MIT Press.

Wagner, Aureen (2008) *CBT for OCD and Anxiety in Children & Adolescents* (workshop).

Webster-Stratton, Carolyn (2006) *The Incredible Years.* Seattle, WA: Incredible Years.

Winner, Michelle (2007) *Thinking about YOU Thinking about ME*, 2nd edition. San Jose, CA: Social Thinking Publishing.

Winner, Michelle (2005) *Think Social! A Social Thinking Curriculum for School-Age Students.* San Jose, CA: Social Thinking Publishing.

Wood, T. Julia (2010) *Interpersonal Communication.* Boston, MA: Wadsworth Cengage Learning.

Index